Be Your Own Brand

Achieve More of What You Want by Being More of Who You Are

David McNally
Karl D. Speak

16

EasyRead Large

RHYW

Copyright Page from the Original Book

Be Your Own Brand

Berrett-Koehler Publishers, Inc.
235 Montgomery Street, Suite 650
San Francisco, California 94104-2916
Tel: (415) 288-0260, Fax: (415) 362-2512
www.bkconnection.com

BK

Ordering information for print editions

Quantity sales. Special discounts are available on quantity purchases by corporations, associations, and others. For details, contact the "Special Sales Department" at the Berrett-Koehler address above.

Individual sales. Berrett-Koehler publications are available through most bookstores. They can also be ordered directly from Berrett-Koehler: Tel: (800) 929-2929; Fax: (802) 864-7626; www.bkconnection.com

Orders for college textbook/course adoption use. Please contact Berrett-Koehler: Tel: (800) 929-2929; Fax: (802) 864-7626.

Orders by U.S. trade bookstores and wholesalers. Please contact Ingram Publisher Services, Tel: (800) 509-4887; Fax: (800) 838-1149; E-mail: customer.service@ingrampublisherservices.com; or visit www.ingram publisherservices.com/Ordering for details about electronic ordering.

Berrett-Koehler and the BK logo are registered trademarks of Berrett-Koehler Publishers, Inc.

Second Edition
Paperback print edition ISBN 978-1-60509-810-4
PDF e-book ISBN 978-1-60509-811-1
IDPF e-book ISBN 978-1-60509-812-8

2011-1

Project management, design, and composition: BookMatters, Berkeley; Copyedit: Natty Kahan; Proofreading: Anne Smith; Index: Leonard Rosenbaum; Cover design: Donna Williams

ReadHowYouWant partners with publishers to provide books for ALL Kinds of Readers. For more information about Becoming A (RHYW) Registered Reader and to find more titles in your preferred format, visit:
<u>www.readhowyouwant.com</u>

TABLE OF CONTENTS

More Praise for Be Your Own Brand

"*Be Your Own Brand* explores the notion of a personal brand not as some kind of scripted performance but as the most genuine and natural affirmation of individual strengths and distinctiveness."

—Matthew Damon, President, Nilan Johnson Lewis

"The explicit and implicit connection between one's personal brand and the brand of the company or organization for whom one works is convincingly presented in this book. Its message—that our brands allow us to become more of who we are, reflecting what we stand for and how we convey that to others—is as true for individuals as it is for organizations."

—Katrinka Smith Sloan, COO, LeadingAge

"*Be Your Own Brand* demonstrates how the principles of marketing can also serve as the foundation of authentic leadership. The authors' ability to draw upon the common understanding of branding to create a parable about self-awareness and effective leadership makes *Be Your Own Brand* essential reading for every manager looking to make a difference."

—Durwin A. Long, PhD, Assistant Dean, Executive and Professional Development, Opus College of Business, University of St. Thomas

"Virtually everyone in business can become a more effective leader by putting into practice the 'power of positive perceptions' presented in this book. In addition, the authors' take on authenticity and making a difference can add a new, powerful perspective to any coach's leadership development activities."

—Karen Gifford, President, Gifford Management and Leadership Coaching

"In the financial services business, the personal brand of each advisor has a big impact on client loyalty. When the personal brand of an advisor is aligned with the company's brand, both become stronger together. The innovative personal brand concepts in *Be Your Own Brand* will help advisors build a stronger personal brand."

—Wick Manley, Senior Vice President, AgStar Financial Services

"The one sales effectiveness book every sales and marketing executive should have on the bookshelf, *Be Your Own Brand* speaks to today's most urgent business issue: your people are your brand.

I found every page to be full of great ideas and powerful insights."

—E. Patrick Gallagher, Director, Learning and Development, FindLaw, a Thomson Reuters Company

"In the financial services industry, a strong personal brand is essential for career success and personal fulfillment. McNally and Speak have written an invaluable guide for helping financial advisors craft such a brand for themselves and their enterprise."

—Michael J. Haglin, Division Vice President, Thrivent Financial for Lutherans

"I saw firsthand how the personal brand concepts in *Be Your Own Brand* were instrumental in helping employees find a strong connection between their work and the value we provided to our customers. The focus on making a difference in the revised version will undoubtedly make these proven concepts of personal brand an even more powerful customer-centric employee engagement tool."

—John Super, President, Advance Path

"As this book says, the brand on the outside is only as good as the brand on the inside. Based on the personal brand concepts in this book, the brand training program we created with Karl helps our associates align their personal brands with our enterprise brand."

—Mark Berryman Hier, Second Vice President, Communications and Research, Securian Financial Group, Inc.

"After reading *Be Your Own Brand,* I only wish that I would have read this book when I started my career as a brand professional sixteen years ago. It's a must-read book for people who wish to achieve their highest level in life. I am currently lecturing in an international university, and this book is mandatory for all my students."

—Dino Martin, Brand Consultant and Associate Faculty Member, Binus University, Jakarta, Indonesia

"Everyone has a brand. This book will teach you how to translate your purpose, vision, and values into a strong personal and professional brand. The book leads you on a journey that will help you understand the power of your personal brand and nurture its evolution throughout your career."

—Agnes Ring, Vice President, Bonestroo

"The personal brand framework concept was introduced to our North America Customer Service Team more than three years ago. Our company's customer satisfaction scores and overall team productivity have increased since we embraced the personal brand alignment framework."

—Barb Kula, Vice President, Marketing, The Mosaic Company

Acknowledgments

Since the first edition of *Be Your Own Brand* was published, one of the strongest personal brands I have ever known passed away. My wife, Jo, the mother of our five children, died in March of 2003. Authenticity defined both who she was and how others perceived her. Today those who knew her still remind me of the difference she made in their lives.

The points of view—the need for authenticity and making a difference as the foundations for building a strong personal brand—emphasized in this revised version of our book have, in fact, not changed from the original. However, that we were "onto something," has been reinforced by the many letters and e-mails we have received from people expressing their appreciation for providing a guide on how to build a strong personal brand without selling your soul.

I have the privilege to be surrounded by strong personal brands whose influence continues to inspire a deep commitment to live my life fully. My children—Sarah, Kate, Sean, Jessie, and Beth—are a whole lot of fun and are passionate about helping make the world a better place for all.

David McNally Sr., my father, now in his late eighties, is still applying his incredible energy and enthusiasm to ensuring that the physically disabled are able to maximize the quality of their lives.

In a world, however, where businesspeople are often thrown together and "branded" as greedy and lacking compassion, I wish to recognize the many leaders who contradict those labels and who are building companies and organizations where the mission, vision, and values are truly lived, and as a result, extraordinary opportunities are created for people to build strong personal brands and live successful and meaningful lives.

Jo Reinhart, my executive assistant, has been an integral part of building my brand for over twenty years. There is not a week that goes by without someone telling me how fortunate I am to have her working with our clients. And finally, in an effort to suggest what is ultimately important, I must acknowledge my golfing brother, Steve, for teaching me how to successfully get out of a bunker and my brother Paul for teaching me to fish.

David McNally

Much of the knowledge that informed this revision of *Be Your Own Brand* came from readers of the first edition of the book and those who have experienced the material in the hundreds and hundreds of workshops that have been conducted globally. I have been inspired by a whole gamut of strong personal brands that I know or observe that reinforce the elegance and power of *being more of who you are, not less.* In that regard, my wife, Beth, the "Steady Eddie" of my life, provided me the support and encouragement to muster the extra-curriculum-like effort to write this revision. Observing my friend Steve Weiss, a quintessential strong personal brand, is a constant reminder of the importance of maintaining high standards for making a difference that separates a strong personal brand from all the others. Sitting in my office on a cold Minnesota winter's day, I received a call out of the blue from Heather Backstrom, a smart, energetic executive coach from California. Heather was adamant that I elevate authenticity as a critical component in building a strong personal brand. Donna Williams, a consummate graphic designer with a whimsical attitude, made the front cover design process a reassuring and enjoyable experience. My daughter, Kathryn, continues her role as the final arbiter of keeping it simple and real for the reader. Sarah Deckenbach has provided vital support in correcting my many keyboarding mistakes, striking what she determines as inappropriate use of commas, and pulling together all of the loose ends in getting the manuscript to the publisher. Finally, my mother with her own brand of encouragement—"Are you done with rewriting that book yet so you can get back to your other work?!"

Karl D. Speak

INTRODUCTION

Being More of Who You Are

Everyone has a brand, and anyone can be a strong brand. It doesn't involve changing your personality—you can be an introvert or extrovert. And it's definitely not about trying to be something you're not. The difference between one personal brand and another is that the person with a *strong brand* utilizes his or her special qualities to make a difference in the lives of others. Read that last sentence again, because it is the foundation upon which a strong personal brand is built. Using one's values and distinctive qualities to make a difference for others is the core ethos of strong, thriving personal brands.

Using marketing techniques merely to create a high profile for oneself is not the point and won't make you a stronger brand. When you make a discernable difference in the life of another, you make a lasting impression and your brand receives credit—a deposit in the "trust bank." Every meaningful impression adds more "credits" that build toward the establishment of a trusting relationship. Since the ability to build trusting relationships is a key component of professional and personal success, people with strong personal brands are able *to achieve more of what they want by being more of who they are.*

One cannot underestimate the importance of authenticity, nor can one overestimate the power of alignment in striving to become a stronger brand. The challenge to building a stronger brand is to have the courage to operate authentically, to strive to find alignment with others, and to be creative in applying one's special qualities to make a difference as often as possible. Passing along these and other "lessons learned" is our motivation for revising *Be Your Own Brand.*

In the first edition of *Be Your Own Brand* we successfully provided the first book that lays out a pragmatic framework for an individual to implement the principles of personal brand. Since writing the first edition, we observed two important trends that have made a big impact on personal brand: The first was the rapid growth and acceptance of personal brand as a professional development framework. The many books written about personal brand that followed *Be Your Own Brand*—some in substance and others in title only—have helped expand its use. The second trend is social media. The introduction and omnipresence of social media has created a tool that enables individuals to build a stronger personal brand in a way hardly imagined when we published the first edition.

After the book was published in 2002, we set out on our separate paths to apply the concepts of personal brand in our different businesses.

Karl, as the principal of Brand Tool Box, Ltd., applied the concepts of personal brand in his capacity as a corporate brand strategist. The pragmatic framework of personal brand allowed Karl to create a useful and powerful foundation for internal brand building. At the core of this corporate brand-building innovation is a framework to align the personal brands of employees with the brand of their corporate employer.

David, as a renowned business speaker and executive coach, employed the framework of personal brand in his business, which is built on inspiring others to thrive through living a purposeful life. David's work in encouraging and coaching individuals to create powerful alignment of their personal brand with the contribution expected of them by their employers resulted in significantly higher employee engagement and commitment to key corporate strategies.

After traveling in our separate circles for years, we got together and compared notes. We observed that people with strong personal brands had a rich network of resources—functional and emotional—that powered the achievement of their goals. Our belief was reinforced that the "formula" for creating a strong personal brand is not complex, however, and that it is clearly a myth that personal brand building involves or requires shameless self-promotion.

Since writing the original edition of *Be Your Own Brand,* we have watched with interest the evolution of the concept of personal brand. In some ways its evolution has mimicked the advancement of the concept of business brand. Slowly (far too slowly in our opinion), companies are realizing that consumers trust a brand (the relationship they have with a product or company) because it consistently provides value and makes a difference for them. Another way of saying that is, *Trust exists because the company or brand delivers on its promises.*

We are even clearer today that this construct also holds true for personal brand. Our practice of adding value and consistently making a difference in the lives of others as the pathway to a strong personal brand is what separates our approach. This stance is the basis for this revision of *Be Your Own Brand.*

In this revised and expanded edition, *Be Your Own Brand* provides you with a contemporary perspective, including the effect of social media on personal brand and a set of tools to help you build a stronger one. We have structured the book in a modular fashion, enabling you to navigate the content in a way that best fits your style. First of all there are three logical sections: "Personal Brand Basics"; "Designing Your Personal Brand of Making a Difference"; and "Using the Power of Alignment to Build a Stronger Personal Brand." Within each of these sections is a set of stand-alone chapters all designed to be a quick read focused on a key element of personal brand building.

Along the way, we will introduce you to a number of interesting individuals who demonstrate how people who dedicate the distinctive qualities of their strong personal brand to making a difference for others build a successful life. You will meet Chip Bell, a great guy who brings a smile to the face of even the grumpiest person. You will also meet Terry Fox, a Canadian hero, who will inspire you with his dedication to making a difference. An introduction to Dr. David Dunn, a prominent world-class surgeon and medical researcher, will demonstrate how a strong personal brand is making a fundamental difference in the global health-care system.

We will introduce you to Temple Grandin—a woman with severe autism since she was a child, who has invented some of the most important improvements in the humane treatment of cattle and was the recent subject of a highly acclaimed HBO film. And you will meet Norman Borlaug, who single-handedly started the Green Revolution and did more than anyone else in the twentieth century to teach the world to feed itself, reducing world hunger on a large scale. And then there's Willem Kolff, a humble Dutch physician who was the pioneer inventor of two important medical devices that have saved millions of lives.

After eight years of helping others understand and embrace the concepts of personal brand, we think we have learned a few things and firmly believe that by sharing them with others the world will benefit from having more strong personal brands. We are hopeful that this is one way we can make a difference, by being more of who we are.

PART I

Personal Brand Basics

1

Personal Brand: The Perception That You Made a Difference

Let's get straight to the point. Everybody already has a brand. Your personal brand is a perception held in others' minds, and it has evolved through their interactions with you. Through repeated contacts between you and another person, his or her perception of you sharpens and your brand in that person's mind becomes clearer. In other words, people are constantly observing who you are, what you do, and how you do it. Having a brand is not the point: more important is the question, How *strong* is your personal brand? The strength of your personal brand grows or weakens depending upon the consistent impact (positive or negative) you are making on other individuals. Want to be a stronger brand? Make a difference!

Ever get the feeling that people—even people who know you (or should know you) very well—just don't "get" you?

Ever get the feeling that the relationships in your life—some of them, anyway—are a little out of sync with your ideals and what you really want?

Ever get the feeling that there's a troubling disconnect—maybe only minor, maybe profound—between your personal life and your professional life?

In every case described above, a gap seems to exist between the "real you" and the you other people see and interact with. At work, at home, in the community, in life in general—it seems that you're not getting as much credit as you feel you deserve for what you contribute and what you truly believe.

The framework of personal brand management set out in this book is designed to enable you to shift others' perceptions so that you can be acknowledged and receive credit for who you are and the difference you make for others. At the base of this framework is a set of simple principles (which we refer to as "personal brand basics"). In this chapter, we will explain two of these three principles: the role of perceptions and the importance of making a difference in relationships.

Understanding these two simple, commonsense principles of personal brand will make it possible for you to immediately start building a stronger brand.

However, before we're off and running, let's make sure we agree on the definition of "personal brand."

A personal brand is a perception or emotion, maintained by somebody other than you, that describes your outstanding qualities and influences that person's relationship with you.

A strong personal brand does not result from a contrived image, colorful clothing, snappy slogan, or from having put on an artificial veneer to disguise the true nature of what's within: A strong personal brand describes a person who chooses to make a meaningful difference in the lives of others and who builds trusting, valued relationships. A weak personal brand describes a person whose attributes and perceived qualities lack clarity, and more importantly, someone who is not perceived to extend him-or herself to make a difference for other people.

What does a personal brand, strong or otherwise, look like? How will people know it when they see it? Think for a moment of someone you know well professionally. How would you describe your relationship with that person? Is this someone with whom you can easily discuss a problem, or someone you'd probably avoid in a sensitive situation? Do you think of them first when you need help or expertise in a particular area, or do they never come to mind? Why does an individual stand out among the hundreds of people in your mental address book?

One of David's colleagues, Sue Stanek, describes how she is consciously evaluating individual personal brands by noticing how she thinks when she passes fellow workers in the office. Looking at one, she might say to herself, "You really make my life easy!" Looking at another, she thinks, "You really make my life difficult." Sue's bottom-line judgments are a reminder of the importance of making a positive difference if you want to be perceived as a strong brand.

Now think about the more intimate relationships in your life, and you'll experience distinct, and often deep, feelings. When you think of your spouse, partner, children, parents, or closest friends, there's a real emotional kick to the mental image, "Oh, that's my dad," "my mom," "the love of my life," "my kids," or "my best buddy from college/the Navy/the team at work." Special relationships have emotions tied to them—that's what makes them so special.

The brands of the important people in your life exist in your mind (just as your brand exists in theirs) based on who you've known them to be and what you've known them to do. Their brand is how you judge them now and how you know what to expect from them the next time you interact. Your perceptions may or may not match what they've consciously worked to create in your mind ... but that's getting a little ahead of our story.

One Really Nice Guy (and a Strong Personal Brand)

For Karl, a good example of a strong personal brand is Dr. Chip R. Bell, who is an author, a trainer, and a consultant. He has a well-developed sense of humor, an engaging Southern drawl, and a depth of expertise that extends from customer service to leadership and the protocols of great partnerships. But most importantly in this context, Chip Bell is a nice guy.

"So what?" you may say. "The world is full of nice guys. Big deal." Chip Bell is a *nice guy who makes a difference.*

Chip Bell embodies an off-the-chart exuberance for life. To anyone who has come within the gravitational pull of his personality, he is the poster boy for contagious enthusiasm. He radiates into a room his active, assertive, outgoing friendliness. A couple of years ago, he and Karl partnered on a consulting road trip in the Pacific Northwest—and Karl still clearly recalls witnessing dimensions of enthusiasm he had never suspected existed.

By his actions and example, Chip Bell inspired Karl—and undoubtedly a lot of other people—to take the personal brand component of optimism and enthusiasm to a whole new level. People do that to us periodically: they take something we believe is one of our own greatest strengths and redefine it right before our eyes, simultaneously transforming it and us.

But why Karl finds Chip Bell such an extraordinary example of a strong personal brand is the sheer genuineness of his behavior—from the moment Chip greets you to the moment you part. When you look into Chip Bell's eyes, he's completely there. In that moment, the connection he makes has a power and a relevance that transcends anything else going on in the room.

Did Chip Bell set out to be the nicest, most enthusiastic guy on the planet? Not at all. He's not engaged in a competitive endeavor, and his effect is not a function of his actions alone. Rather, Chip Bell values friendliness—values it extremely highly—and that, in turn, dictates his outgoing, involved behavior.

It's an amazing thing to stand next to and watch Chip Bell. He has no self-consciousness, no sense of pretense or artifice. In other words, Chip Bell's authenticity (a word we'll come back to at some length in chapter 4) is so apparent that its impact on others is immediate and lasting. Chip Bell's brand of exuberance and passion for life rubs off on other people and changes their day—and maybe their perspective on life. Chip Bell is an excellent example of a strong personal brand.

Your values and habits may not be the same as Chip Bell's. Nor should they be, if his brand doesn't contribute to an accurate reflection of who you are. But when you can indelibly imprint yourself on the mind of someone else, you've arrived as a strong personal brand.

It's fair to say that most people have a similar perception of Chip Bell, and that's the beginning of being a strong brand. The other quality that makes him such a strong brand is that he uses his distinctive qualities to make a difference for others as often as possible. This brings us to linking the first principle, the power of perceptions, to the second principle, making a difference. (The third principle will be the subject of chapter 2.) The remainder of this chapter is dedicated to providing you a practical understanding of these two important concepts.

"It Isn't What They Say About You, It's What They Whisper"—Errol Flynn

When it comes to your personal brand, what *you* think doesn't matter, but what *other people* think matters a whole lot. Your brand exists on the basis of a set of perceptions and emotions stored in someone else's head.

The good and bad news about how others perceive you is that once locked in place, perceptions have tremendous staying power.

Perception is reality. Sound familiar? Most people have heard this simple aphorism. Yet it is reasonable to assume that although many people understand that other people have certain perceptions about them, too few people make the effort to proactively manage the perceptions they leave with others. Why is that? Some people are confident they will leave the right impression. Other individuals feel it is too difficult to influence what others think. And still other people claim they don't care about what others think of them. Frankly, we know from asking thousands of people—they're not sure exactly what perceptions they want to leave.

An important competency of building and growing a strong personal brand is to harness the power of perceptions. If others' perceptions define our personal brand, we need to be purposeful about managing the perceptions we leave with them. Let's be clear that how people perceive us has a significant impact on how they relate to, and react to, us. And, in some cases, their perceptions may impact whether they will even take the time to meet with us. So, to leverage our personal brand and make the most of our relationships, we must improve our competency of managing the perceptions we create.

Even with our best intentions of managing others' perceptions of us, it is not easy. Commonly we view ourselves one way while others have a very different perception of us. Can you imagine, or do you know, someone who takes pride at being a hard worker—while other people perceive him or her as a workaholic? Who's right? How does that difference in perceptions impact their relationship? How about the person who is proud of being well informed but who others see as a know-it-all? Whose point of view matters more? In the end, the perspective others have of us will clearly bias how they perceive and relate to us.

There are many reasons why a difference exists between how one perceives oneself and how one is perceived by others. We each have a unique set of lenses through which we view others, so to speak. Each person's lenses are colored by life's experiences, attitudes at the time, and how the person feels about him-or herself at a particular moment. The result is that a person's actions or words may be interpreted differently by various other people or at different times. Building a strong brand requires a level of wisdom and flexibility to ensure that one's actions and words consistently reinforce the way one wants to be perceived. No one said building a strong personal brand didn't take some effort!

Misperceptions can also result from a certain plan of action not turning out as intended. Now let us give you an example: A young lady (Sally) in her early twenties went home to her mom and told her that she and her fiancé wanted to save some money to buy a house before getting married. She asked her mom if she could move back home to save money, and her mom said, "Well, how long will you be here?" Sally looked disappointed because she took her mom's comment to mean she wasn't welcome back home. Mom was thinking that if Sally would be home for a minimum of six months, Mom could put her back on the family's car insurance and save her daughter even more money. But that's not the perception Sally was left with, and it took time to reassure her that her mom understood her situation and wanted to help.

The third point to keep in mind about perceptions is that people sometimes base them on our actions and other times by what they judge as our intentions. In either case, perceptions are what matter. Perceptions define our brands. And we all must hold ourselves accountable to the perceptions we leave—not to our intentions or solely the actions we take.

So what's the bottom line, and why should anyone work so hard to manage the perceptions others have of them? It's all about the gap: The size of the gap between the way you want to be perceived and the way you are perceived by another person will have a big impact on the general tenor and productivity of the relationship. A narrower gap supports a productive and enjoyable relationship. Conversely, a wider gap results in a relationship that will require more effort to accomplish things, and interacting may not be as much fun.

It's Not About Being Different, It's About the Difference You Make

The second principle of personal brand is centered on the importance of using your special qualities to make a difference. Strong personal brands thrive by finding ways to contribute and make a positive difference for others. Although this concept is uncomplicated, we explain it because it is a most important principle to understand.

The perceptions others have of you are directly related to how much of a difference you make for them. The bigger the difference—positive or negative—the longer the perception remains in their minds. When you make little or no difference for someone, his or her perception of you evaporates faster than you might think. Think of how many people you have interacted with over the past two weeks. How many can you recall? How clear or complete are your perceptions of them? It's safe to say that the number of people you remember and the number who left you with a clear set of perceptions is a fraction of your total interactions. How many people would recall their interactions with you because you made a discernable difference?

It's a Whole New Social Networked World

Social media, as we know it today, was nonexistent when *Be Your Own Brand* was first published. It is a huge understatement to say social media has profoundly changed the way people interact and relate to other people. In a personal brand context, this brave new world greatly impacts the way people make impressions and are perceived by others. The social networked world has added a new dimension to building and managing a personal brand and the perceptions that define it. In this revision of *Be Your Own Brand,* we provide critical insights about how to use the power of social media to build a stronger personal brand.

For starters, a myriad of different tools exist (e.g., Facebook, Twitter, LinkedIn, blogs, Flickr, YouTube, MySpace, Ning, Classmates.com, Friendster, orkut, Multiply, and Match.com , to name only a few) to represent your personal brand in the social media world. The many and diverse social media tools allow you to broaden the awareness of your brand across a much larger audience, with many different segments. These tools vastly transcend the possibilities of extending your personal brand across many audiences in the real world (by which we mean the nonvirtual, not-online world). Using a portfolio of social media tools to proactively extend your personal brand offers exciting brand-building opportunities and, of course, challenges.

Hyperlinking, tagging, linking within networks, social bookmarking, SEO strategies, sharing, and becoming "friends" are all examples of tools that catapult and enormously expand the potential for creating perceptions of your personal brand in the social media world. Ideally, people self-direct and manage the power of social media tools to grow their personal brand. But experience suggests that world is not so clean or controlled. Perceptions of your brand can be influenced by someone else—and without your permission.

There has always been gossip in the real world, but the social media world is gossip on steroids! Then there is guilt by association, so to speak. One of personal brand management's axioms is "Your brand is known by the company it keeps." It is a lot easier for people to "associate" with you, and without you knowing it, in the social media world.

The other potential of using social media tools is the enormous number of extra possibilities to make a difference for someone. Sometimes with only a few keystrokes you can contribute something of value to someone else. Because of the power of the linked network, you may have a chance to encourage, empower, assist, or help to make a difference for someone you have never even met.

The social media world offers opportunities (and some pitfalls) to building a stronger brand than was ever imagined when we first created the concept of personal brand. We provide specific examples and suggestions for using social media tools and strategies to build a stronger brand in chapter 9.

Feelings Create Lasting Perceptions

"I've learned that people will forget what you said, people will forget what you did, but people will never forget how you made them feel."

This profound aphorism attributed to Maya Angelou has real, important meaning for personal brand building. When you make a truly positive impact on another person, you leave them with a warm feeling. Strong feelings create lasting memories. Making a positive and distinctive difference for someone is the surest way to become a strong brand.

2

A Strong Personal Brand Delivers on Three Important Expectations

Do the people you know perceive qualities in you that are truly distinctive? Do they believe that you make those qualities relevant to them and their needs? Are they convinced that you will demonstrate those qualities consistently? If you can confidently answer yes to all three of these questions, you can expect to reap the benefits of having a strong brand with those people.

Most of us can answer yes to all three with some people in our lives. But how many? Is your network of strong personal brand relationships large enough to help you achieve what is important to you?

Three key components combine to determine the strength of your brand. These components combined form the third fundamental principle of personal brand. Strong brands are perceived to be:

Distinctive: They stand for something. They have a point of view.

Relevant: What they stand for connects to what someone else considers to be important.

Consistent: People come to believe in a relationship based on the consistency of behaviors they experience or observe.

Taken together, these characteristics create value and trust in a relationship—the core definition of a strong brand. Simply stated, the math goes something like this: when someone believes that you make your distinctive qualities relevant to them, the value you bring to the relationship is clearly established (i.e., you made a difference); when you are consistent in creating value, people know they can trust you to add value time and time again.

Strong Personal Brands Are Distinctive

Your brand starts to become strong when you decide what you believe in and then commit to acting on those beliefs. At that very point, you begin to separate yourself from the crowd. Here's why—making a commitment means doing what you said you would do despite the obstacles. Since your beliefs are not always shared by another, standing up for and holding to them is often a courageous act—and courage of this kind is not too common in our world. That, by definition, is distinctive.

Since the first edition of *Be Your Own Brand* was published, thousands of people have been surveyed to find out which of these qualities—distinctive, relevant, or consistent—is the most difficult to achieve. The majority of respondents indicate that being perceived to be distinctive is the least difficult. This is a common misconception. Most people underestimate what it takes to be perceived to be distinctive in some way. Moreover, being perceived as distinctive can make many people feel uncomfortable. It takes considerable effort and internal fortitude to be perceived to be distinctive. For example, if you believe one of your outstanding qualities is that you are a caring person, are you willing to demonstrate your caring nature in front of people who might disagree with, and be highly critical of, your actions?

To truly understand what it means to be distinctive is to learn that it implies much more than merely being different. Brand building is not image building. It is not selling yourself to someone else. It results from understanding the needs of others, wanting to meet those needs, and being able to do so while staying true to your values.

As we'll see in greater detail in chapter 4, clarifying, understanding, and acting on the basis of values is a core building block in the art of developing a strong personal brand. For now, suffice it to say that your values are the beliefs you hold to be true and the principles by which you live your life—all of which influence how you prioritize competing demands.

Your values affect not only what you think and feel, but also how you behave. How you act on your values is what distinguishes you from the crowd. As people observe your actions, they make judgments about why you do what you do. Those judgments then become the perception of you they carry around with them. The more distinctive your actions, the clearer their perceptions and the better defined your brand becomes for them. In other words, personal brands grow strong when they are focused on meeting the needs of others without sacrificing the values on which they are based.

We cannot emphasize enough that building a strong personal brand takes much more than looking good, finding the right logo or stationery, or even designing an eye-popping website. While those things may bring attention to you, your brand will ultimately be a reflection of the ideas and values that are distinctively you. This is the only substance upon which a truly lasting relation-ship can be built. The lesson:

Your personal brand is based on your values, not the other way around.

Strong Personal Brands Are Relevant

Being distinctive is not the only thing that matters to someone else. What you stand for needs to be relevant to them.

Relevance begins when a person believes that you understand and care about what's important to them. It gains strength every time you demonstrate that what's important to them is important to you. The synergistic effect of being both distinctive and relevant is what ignites the power of a personal brand. It takes wisdom, insight, empathy, intuition, and often extra effort to be relevant to another person.

Relevance is also a function of circumstances. Parents are naturally relevant to their children, for they are the caregivers and protectors of those children. The relevance of one spouse to another extends far beyond the bonds of a marriage contract: the actual relevance occurs when both people in the marriage are concerned about and committed to each other's well-being.

Relevance is what distinguishes a friend from an acquaintance. A coworker may be relevant only to the degree that what they do affects what you do, whereas a mentor's support and interest in your career and future makes that relationship far more valued and lasting than an ordinary relationship with a fellow employee. Your relevance to your clients or customers is determined not only by your product or service, but by how it (and you) can proficiently solve their problems and meet their needs. The more relevance you demonstrate, the stronger your brand becomes to them. Relevance is what makes strong brands continue to attract attention and stand out from the crowd.

Building relevance involves a skill we call "thinking in reverse." If you want to be considered valuable to others, you must move out of your world into theirs. Your first concern is to determine their needs and interests. Then you connect those needs and interests to your own personal strengths and abilities. The sages throughout the ages have said in many different ways: "Before you can get what you want, you must first help others get what they want."

That means relevance is a process. It starts with questions. What do they want? What do they need? What do they value? What do they expect? When you have a sense of someone else's needs and frame of reference, that information allows you to guide your actions in ways that will make you relevant. The best salespeople are highly skilled—and in some cases intuitive—about discovering what is relevant to a prospective buyer. To ensure their success, the salesperson discovers what is of the utmost importance to a prospect in terms of his or her needs and problems before presenting ideas. Targeting comments or solutions toward the issues that are relevant to the particular prospect allows that person to see clearly the value the salesperson brings to the relationship.

There is a strong aspirational element to being truly relevant to others. Webster's defines "aspiration" as "a strong desire to achieve something high or great." Most people would be pleased to hear that someone described them as a "great person." But people don't tend to hand out that label randomly. The lesson:

Relevance is something we earn by the importance others place on what we do for them and by their judgment of how well we do it.

Strong Personal Brands Are Consistent

The third component in building a strong brand is consistency—doing things that are both distinctive and relevant, and doing them again and again and again. Consistency is a hallmark of all strong brands. As a brand, you only get "credit" (acknowledgment, acceptance, or recognition by others) for what you do consistently. Consistent behaviors define your brand more clearly and concisely than the most polished and practiced patter. Consistency requires the discipline to overcome circumstances, personal feelings, and frankly, some of the spin and hyperbole that is often thrown at us.

In the American public's consciousness—even for people who have never met them and may not like or even agree with them—figures such as Martha Stewart, Oprah Winfrey, Rush Limbaugh, Sarah Palin, Lou Holtz, Warren Buffet, Bono, and countless others stand as strong personal brands based on the consistency of their actions. In other countries and cultures, the list of names changes, but the stature doesn't.

Which strongly branded public figures an individual labels admirable and which ones they label not so admirable will vary based on point of view. Everyone defines distinctiveness in his or her own terms. Each public figure's relevance to your needs and values will also vary. But like them or not, need them or not, you feel you know what to expect from these people because their behavior has been so consistent over so many years.

In a relationship, consistency is established by dependability of behavior. Over time, people learn that they can trust you if they experience consistent, trustworthy behaviors. In the absence of personal experience, they may decide to trust you because of what they have learned of your track record from others. Your previous actions—not your intentions—lead them to believe that you can be counted on to behave in a similar way again. And every time you behave the way they expect, you reinforce the strength of your brand with them. Trust grows.

Conversely, the quickest way to diminish and ultimately destroy someone's trust is to become inconsistent. No matter how high the highs may have been, roller-coaster behavior will work against the long-term prospects of any relationship. The lesson:

Consistency is the hallmark of all strong personal brands. *Inconsistency weakens brands and suspends belief.*

The Power of Example

Some people live decades and never really achieve a lasting impact on the people around them. Some leave a lasting legacy based on a few short years. The latter group has brands that stand the test of time, even though time itself is denied to them in any great amount.

An excellent example is Canadian Terry Fox, who was the subject of David's award-winning film, *The Power of Purpose.* At the age of eighteen, Terry Fox was diagnosed with bone cancer. His right leg was amputated six inches above the knee, and he spent a long time in the hospital in recovery and rehabilitation. While there, he was moved by the suffering he saw all around him—so moved that he decided to do something about it. Three years after losing his leg, he vowed to run across Canada to raise money for cancer research. His goal: Raise at least one dollar for every man, woman, and child in the country—over $24 million.

He started in mid-April, dipping his artificial foot in the Atlantic Ocean. During the next 143 days, initial casual interest turned into a national phenomenon. Terry Fox was running 42 kilometers (over 25 miles) a day. On September 1, just east of Thunder Bay, Ontario—two-thirds of the way to the Pacific and over 5,300 kilometers from his starting point—his run came to a premature end. His cancer had returned. He died the following June, one month before his twenty-third birthday.

Terry Fox lived, however, to see what many had described as the "impossible" fundraising goal of $24 million reached and exceeded. He raised $28 million.

Those who knew Terry were quick to say that he was no saint. But he showed tremendous integrity about why he was running and what the money he raised was going for, and he would not let anyone muddy the waters. He made sure that all his expenses were covered by sponsorships or contributions so every dollar donated actually went to cancer research. He made every step count.

That was in 1980. Today, Terry Fox Runs are held in more than thirty countries, from Albania to Zimbabwe. The extraordinary legacy he left—directed now by the Terry Fox Foundation in Toronto, Ontario—has raised more than half a billion dollars for cancer research. In 1999, a national survey conducted by the Dominion Institute and the Council for Canadian Unity found that in the minds of his countrymen, Terry Fox is Canada's greatest hero.

Is Terry Fox a strong brand? Let's look at the criteria: Is he distinctive? Yes. Has he made his distinctive qualities relevant to others? Yes. Is he consistent? Yes. Has he made a difference? No doubt!

Our journeys through life may not be as dramatic as Terry Fox's; but when our values lead to distinctive, relevant, and consistent actions, the effects we have on the world around us can transcend the limits of time and place and transform the lives of others.

Climbing the Brand Ladder

Because of the dynamic nature of a relationship, the process of being distinctive, relevant, and consistent has some subtle shading. Each interaction builds on the one before it and sets the stage for the one that will follow. As the relationship deepens and grows, it acquires a history—a breadth and depth that takes on increasing significance over time.

When you look back to your first experiences with someone important in your life, do you find yourself marveling at how little you knew about each other? From the perspective of time and experience, you can see that your relationship now exists at a much higher level. It's as though you'd been climbing a ladder, with each rung taking your relationship to a new level.

In business, the concept of brand ladders is used to determine how—through repeated encounters—distinctive product and service features connect with the relevant emotional needs and values of customers. The purpose is to develop depth and breadth in the relationship. Each step leads to another, gradually getting closer to the emotional core that makes for enduring relationships.

When you open a checking account, your brand-based expectations for choosing one bank over another are likely to be pretty simple: "Keep my money safe for me until I need it. Send me a clear, accurate statement periodically. Be open for enough hours and in enough locations to make it convenient for me to do business with you."

Those are lower rungs on the bank's brand ladder. But then one day you need something more—a mortgage, a loan for a new car, or a savings program for the kids' college fund. Now the bank's brand connection has a chance to move up your emotional ladder. You likely place a different—and significantly higher—value on your home or your children's future than you do on your checking account. As the bank justifies your trust at this higher level, the brand connection moves up a rung.

The same dynamic works on a personal scale as well. You start by finding out what is initially distinctive and relevant to other people in your life. What are their values and beliefs? What do they stand for? What do they need from others in a relationship? What, in particular, do they need from you in the beginning stages of your relationship?

The brand connection grows as you use this knowledge to progressively work your way up their ladder of ideas, desires, and values. The experience and insight you gain as you move up the scale allows you to better understand the higher-level benefits and emotional rewards they derive from connecting with you consistently. First contacts often are tentative: neither person involved is quite sure what to expect. As our relationships move to higher levels of emotional connection, we seem to instinctively know what someone needs from us, and often we don't have to think twice to provide it.

When a mother or father asks a child at dinner, "Is your food okay?" they want to make sure things taste right. That's a lower rung on the brand ladder of "parent." But an enthusiastic—especially an unsolicited—"Wow, this is really good. Thanks!" says a lot more than that the meal is okay. It says that the child values the time spent on his or her behalf, which makes Mom or Dad feel appreciated. That's a higher step on the ladder.

When that feeling of being appreciated is relevant to what people believe are their responsibilities, a much higher level of connection has been achieved. Their values are reinforced—which means that, in our example, finding the time to be together at mealtimes is likely to continue to be an important part of building the relationship between parent and child.

Some Reflections on Building Your Brand

Because of the back-and-forth nature of a relation- ship, a commitment to being distinctive and relevant to others has important carryover effects for you. Determining ways to be relevant to others reflects your desire to learn and grow. This, in turn, is expressed by continually creating meaningful connections, solving problems, and making things better for others and yourself.

But because others determine whether or not you're effective at brand building, your relevance to them is ultimately their decision. And sometimes the connection simply won't be there. You won't always get along with everybody. You can't. Nobody can. Your values, however distinctive, simply won't appeal to everyone. Neither will they be relevant to everyone. You can't be all things to all people, nor should you try to be.

So one key determination you need to make in building your brand is how relevant specific other people are, or can be, to you. If you're going to be true to yourself and be acknowledged, accepted, and recognized for who you really are, your core values must be respected in each relationship, not compromised. To think you will never leave someone dissatisfied runs counter to the idea of a strong personal brand. So you also must decide if a particular relationship is worth the effort.

Clarity in relationships is a key advantage of a strong personal brand. As your brand becomes better defined, people find it easier to figure out where you stand and, consequently, what value you can represent for them. They'll learn to respect your values because it will be clearer to them that those values are of utmost importance to you. As a result, they won't expect you to act in a way that contradicts those values. The payoff for you is that the number of conflicts in your life will likely diminish.

Strong vs. Moral

Personal brand is not the same thing as morality in the spiritual sense—though there are, to be sure, a lot of common elements. Personal brands are not good or bad. There are strong and weak brands. In essence, a strong brand signifies a person who has clearly chosen values and is recognized for the difference he or she makes for others. A weak brand would be a label for a person who shows ambivalence about what he or she stands for and doesn't exert much effort to make a difference for others. Everyone knows people who have clearly defined brands as well as character traits and behavior patterns we (or others) may find anything from mildly distasteful to absolutely horrifying.

Think, for example, of the recently deceased and infamous convicted mobster John Gotti. Strong brand? Absolutely. People who knew him knew exactly what he stood for, what his values were, and how he could be counted on to act in a given situation. Did that make his brand attractive? To some people (those to whom his distinctive actions and values were consistently relevant), yes. To most, no. In essence, it was strong for all the wrong reasons. But in selected relationships, he clearly established a strong personal brand.

Stand for Your Brand

Not all brands are attractive to us. Your values are your values. Our values are ours. We won't presume to judge them against a universal scale of right or wrong. Figuring out the "right thing" for you—that's your job.

But, when your actions and your behavior reflect your values, the result is integrity. The pieces fit. The picture you present to others is in focus, not blurred around the edges or incomplete. As stated above, we'll come back to values clarification at greater length in chapter 4. For now, though, it is vital to appreciate that acting in concert with your values not only affects your relationships with others, it also has a highly positive effect on your relationship with yourself.

For purposes of this analysis, the "right way" to go about building a strong personal brand is to make sure your brand resonates and is relevant, in the most distinctive way possible, for those people with whom you want to build strong relationships on a long-term basis. The "wrong way" is to not develop a distinctive, relevant, consistent brand at all—to base your behaviors on inconsistent, ever-shifting values that aren't clear to you or anyone else.

As noted earlier, building a strong personal brand takes discipline—because consistency takes discipline. You not only need to be clear about what you believe, you also need to be willing to base your actions on those beliefs time after time, no matter how great the temptation may be to compromise them. The way to make a distinctive, enduring, positive impression on someone else is to ensure that who you are, what you say you are, and what that person experiences from you are the same, time and time again.

3

Your Personal Brand Is Perceived from Three Different Dimensions

Earlier in our time together we talked about the importance of creating and managing the perceptions others have of you. Admittedly, the notion of perceptions can be a bit nebulous, and understanding how those perceptions come together to define your personal brand can appear daunting. In this chapter, we will explain a simple and proven model that you can use to master the management of these perceptions.

The role of perceptions is one of the most similar aspects between business and personal brand—it is one of the elements of business brand that has a clear translation to personal brand. Dissatisfied with the complexity so often found in other approaches to understanding brand perceptions, Karl's company, Brand Tool Box, has invested over $2 million to date in market research to validate a simplified model of brand perceptions that is now helping a growing number of businesses effectively define their brands.

In many ways the translation was straightforward, but in other ways we needed to make modifications to ensure that the business-based version could be used as a model for personal brand. Since the first edition of *Be Your Own Brand,* the perceptions model of personal brand has proven to be a practical and effective tool.

Changing the Focus

In chapter 2, we showed you that from the vantage point of someone else, your brand takes shape as a result of your ability to make what you do distinctive, relevant, and consistent to that person. The Brand Tool Box Personal Brand Model™ (to which we turn our attention now) is designed to show you what you look like to someone else—what specific attributes go into the image of your brand they carry around in their mind. Later on we will show you how to use the Personal Brand Model as the cornerstone of your personal brand platform, a framework for building your brand.

In over twenty years of working with businesses in a variety of industries and market situations, our experience suggests that people connect to a brand through three interrelated dimensions: competencies, standards, and style. For personal branding, the model above combines these three distinct but interrelated dimensions in a similar fashion:

It identifies your brand roles: The first brand dimension refers to the basic nature of the relationship and what you need to do capably merely to meet someone's basic expectations. It might help to think of this in terms of the role (or combination of roles) you play for a particular person: for example, friend or neighbor, parent or boss, mechanic or physician.

It establishes your brand standards: The idea of a competent parent or friend or mechanic is somewhat generic. The second brand dimension begins to make your brand image much more specific by focusing on the way you *deliver* your roles. Your brand standards are the level of performance that you are willing to adhere to consistently.

FIGURE 1. Personal Brand Model Brand Tool Box Personal Brand Model © 1989–2008 Brand Tool Box, Ltd.

It displays your brand style: The third dimension is the manner in which you communicate and interact with others. This is how we personalize our roles within the context of our performance standards. Think of brand style as the emotional image developed—not only through first impressions, but from repeated contacts—as you interact with others.

As a relationship evolves and grows, these dimensions also will evolve, but in different ways.

The roles at the heart of the relationship will usually remain relatively constant over time. Change here will typically be progressive and incremental in nature.

Standards tend to become more defined as experience clarifies expectations. Change here will involve greater precision and accuracy as we learn in greater detail what someone else needs from us.

Style changes will reflect a growing level of familiarity, even intimacy. As each person in the relationship gains an ever better sense of what behaviors will best maintain, nurture, and deepen the connection between them, continuing adjustments here cement the bond.

You're always a parent, in other words, but the standards needed to effectively parent a three-year-old child and a thirteen-year-old child are vastly different. In a work setting, the same principle applies to managing a twenty-six-year-old employee and a forty-six-year-old employee. The standards you'll apply to your actions also change as your child grows and develops or the relationship with your employee matures. And through the years, your style of parenting or leadership will be crystallized in the countless encounters between you and your child or you and your employee.

The Look of a Personal Brand

To see how roles, standards, and style interrelate, consider the relationship between a parent and a child. There are billions of such relationships, each one unique, but most involve some common characteristics.

Being a parent in the general sense suggests certain forms of competencies (abilities or skills) that come with the role: being a counselor, guide, caregiver, mentor, and so forth.

When you tighten the focus to your own father or mother, that foundation of competencies supports a sense of specific standards (levels of performance) displayed by your particular parents. They had their own way of handling family time, setting rules, helping with homework, preparing meals, defining limits, providing discipline, planning vacations, handing out allowances, and the like. It wasn't quite the same as the way your friends' parents did things, but the different approaches still fit under the role of parent.

Beyond those things, however, there's also a rich vein of emotional experience that comes to mind when you think of your parents' particular style of behavior. Their tone of voice, their attitudes, their facial expressions and body language—all go well beyond what they did, to define a special style of doing it. Their style dimensions tend to involve highly subjective descriptions: upbeat or cynical, always in a hurry or very reflective, conservative or a little wacky, warm and loving or reserved and controlled.

Taken together, the unique combination of roles, standards, and style demonstrated to you over the years by your parents—and modified by how you reacted and interacted with them—defines a unique and memorable relationship in your life. It's a "branded" relationship. It may have much in common with the parent-child relationships your friends recall or that you have with your own children. But nonetheless it's different, personal, and anything but a generic experience.

The way you communicate and act when you do what you do (your style) and the norms within which you consistently operate (your standards) allow you to meet some basic needs of someone else (your roles) in each meaningful relationship in your life. When your brand is clearly defined and strongly maintained, the result is an impression as distinctive and uniquely personal as a fingerprint.

Let's examine each part of the Personal Brand Model in more detail.

Roles: Our Relationship with Others

In business, when consumers think about a brand—whether it represents a product, a service, a company, or an employer—often they first describe it based on what it does for them. A car, for example, regardless of how it was built (standards) or how it looks (style), must start, move, stop, keep the rain out, and keep the passengers in (competencies). A meal, regardless of how it was cooked (standards) or arranged on the plate (style), must be palatable and bear a reasonable resemblance to what the customer ordered (competencies).

FIGURE 2. Personal Brand Roles Brand Tool Box Personal Brand Model © 1989–2008 Brand Tool Box, Ltd.

Building a strong personal brand starts from a similar base. Your roles are the fundamental reason you are in a particular relationship with another person: father or mother, sister or brother, boss,

40

- Speaker
- Writer
- Father
- Husband

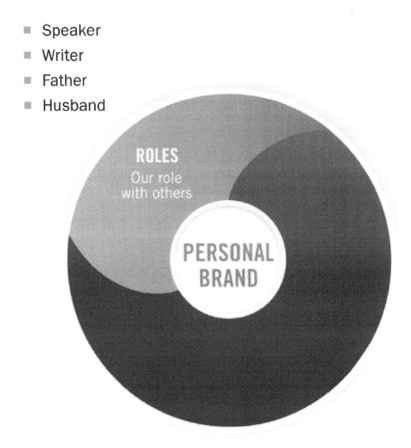

FIGURE 3. Chip Bell's Personal Brand Roles Brand Tool Box
Personal Brand Model © 1989–2008 Brand Tool Box, Ltd.

attorney, friend, financial or spiritual advisor, spouse or former spouse, nurse, mechanic, etc. An expectation on the part of the other person that you are, or can be, competent forms the basis for the relationship.

McDonald's and Wendy's both make hamburgers very competently. Although they may have successfully differentiated themselves in the public's minds based on standards and style, their basic competencies are very similar—preparing and serving hot food in a clean setting at a value price. They must be able to do those things just to be in the hamburger business.

If they can't cook, dress, and wrap a burger—or the place is perceived as unhealthy or the cost of doing what they do is higher than someone will pay (or the price they charge so low that it doesn't cover their cost of doing business)—they won't last.

Similarly, before you can begin to make your personal brand distinctive, you must ensure that you have demonstrated to the person with whom you want a relationship that you can competently meet his or her baseline needs and desires. A prospective heart surgeon who faints at the sight of blood or an apprentice electrician who can't seem to grasp the importance of not sticking metal tools into live outlets has little chance of succeeding. If you can't establish your roles, differentiation will never get to be an issue, because the fundamental foundation of the relationship will never be established or will quickly fall apart.

Remember Chip Bell from chapter 1? The roles part of his Personal Brand Model (as we would diagram in figure 3): You can see that he relates to different people in different ways—as a speaker, writer, father, husband, and so forth. Before his infectious enthusiasm can begin to differentiate him in someone else's mind, he must demonstrate his ability to competently do what needs to be done in each relationship setting.

To develop a strong personal brand, begin by identifying the nature of the key relationships you plan to have. You must be insightful and realistic about the types of relationships that will support your journey to success, and clearheaded in your assessment of your own ability and willingness to offer the roles required.

Remember, however, that regardless of how you assess your roles, in the final analysis it's the "customer"—the all-important other party in the relationship—who sets the bar for you. You can't control others' perceptions, but you can and do guide people to see you as you want to be seen, based on your knowledge of what they need and want from you in a relationship. The deeper the relationship, the more your mutual understanding grows.

Standards: How You Do It

If roles are the noun part of a brand, standards and style are the modifiers—the descriptive adverbs and adjectives that create a uniquely detailed picture of your brand in someone's mind. Standards often are measurable or can be defined somewhat objectively.

Examples of Personal Brand Standards

Nonjudgmental listener
Proficient networker
Consistent values
Reliably efficient
Open-minded/flexible
Consensus-oriented
Assertively opinionated

Focused on a closed circle of contacts
Situational values
Creatively undisciplined
Straight/orthodox
Independent and self-directed

FIGURE 4. Personal Brand Standards Brand Tool Box Personal
Brand Model © 1989–2008 Brand Tool Box, Ltd.

As you can see from the difference between the
left column and the right column, standards that can
be positive and attractive to one person might be
considered negative, even off-putting, to another.
That's the nature of relationships—different strokes
for different folks. The needs of the relationship define

which standards will be considered appropriate or inappropriate.

The point is not to constantly change your standards of behavior in a manic quest to try to please everybody, no matter how different their needs and expectations or how incompatible their values and yours. Focus your standards on the relationships you choose to build with people who truly matter to you.

Your standards significantly influence how others perceive you. Far beyond the basic form of roles involved in the relationship, standards begin to define and give substance to the strength of your personal brand. Consequently, even though your roles in a given area may be the same as many others', your brand standards help you stand out from the crowd.

For example, if you want people to perceive you as really committed to doing a great job, what are your standards on quality? Are you prepared to make sure that every detail is covered, however long it takes, or have you focused on those details most essential to getting the job done? The "however long it takes" attention to detail that might delight one person could drive another over the edge.

Similarly, are you a take-charge person, more directive when it comes to solving problems, or do you hold back and let others try to work things out for themselves? Are you flexible in your approaches or highly systematic? Are you high priced or budget based? Highly tolerant or very demanding? High maintenance or low stress? Technologically adept or not?

In a given situation, different people will respond in different ways. It's up to the person to whom they're responding to determine the standards that are distinctive and relevant to their needs. If you're prepared to provide behavior that matches the other person's standards of distinctiveness and relevance, the relationship is worth developing. Otherwise, you have to decide whether perhaps it isn't the right fit for you, or whether your standards need to change to create a better fit.

Examining standards holds up a very useful—but not always flattering—mirror. For example, if you want your boss, subordinates, colleagues, or coworkers to perceive you as being on the cutting edge in a given area, how much time do you set aside for personal research and development? You might say you have competencies in a given area, but until you demonstrate those competencies in a distinctive and relevant way on a consistent basis, you can't expect to be given full credit for your claim.

Similarly, if you want to be valued for a strong personal brand at home, what is your level of investment in your relationships with your spouse and children? How much of your time, talent, and attention do you give them? If you want your friends to know they can count on you, what evidence do they have upon which to base that judgment? How do you define being there for them? Is that the level of performance they expect and need?

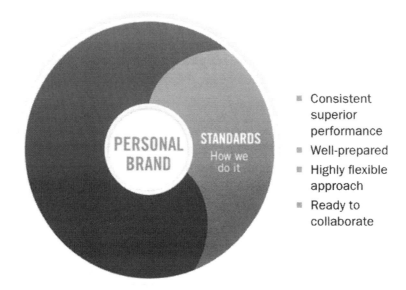

FIGURE 5. Chip Bell's Personal Brand Standards Brand Tool Box Personal Brand Model © 1989–2008 Brand Tool Box, Ltd.

To build a strong personal brand, it's critical to recognize that people cannot see your intentions—they can only see your actions. But from their perceptions of those actions, they make judgments about your standards as well as your roles—not only about what you do, but how well you choose to do it.

Figure 5 is what Chip Bell's Personal Brand Model looks like with standards added. It is important to note that there can be some crossover between standards and style. Being professional sets a standard of performance, but it's also a recognizable style of behavior. Note also that the idea of being a nice guy still doesn't really appear. That's more specifically a style—and that comes next.

Style: How You Relate

Style is your brand's personality. It's the subjective counterpart to the more objective attributes of standards—the part that makes you uniquely yourself in someone else's mind.

Often the words people use to describe style elements will have a strong emotional tinge: friendly, easygoing, intense, aggressive, professional, fun, energetic, introverted, extroverted, controlling, free-spirited, open, or biased. It's not uncommon, in fact, for people to describe different brands in their lives (people and their experiences with them) strictly in terms of style. We say someone is really fun. They're whimsical. They're stodgy. They're flexible. They're arrogant. They're happy. They're conservative. They're creative. Although we may regard these as descriptions of a personality, they are also essentially style components.

Note that these words tend to be subjective, not overtly measurable. Yet because a strong brand builds an emotional connection, they can carry just as much weight as more quantifiable standards. Here's where a lot of the "coloring" in a relationship comes in. Style cannot have real impact or significantly contribute to the building of a strong personal brand, however, unless the other two dimensions—roles and standards—are firmly established.

FIGURE 6. Personal Brand Style Brand Tool Box Personal Brand Model © 1989–2008 Brand Tool Box, Ltd.

Figure 7 shows Chip Bell's completed Personal Brand Model. Now, subjective characteristics like enthusiasm and energy can take his personal brand from a basic level of roles with professional performance standards to a vibrant, uniquely memorable brand image based on an indelibly imprinted style.

When we assemble the Personal Brand Model of an individual like Chip Bell, you can start to see how the pieces interlock and strengthen each other. Roles are the foundation upon which you begin to build your brand. Taken alone, however, your roles may be quite similar to those of many other people. Roles are a starting point, but they don't provide differentiation. That comes from standards and style.

The Personal Brand Model was created as a practical tool for individuals to improve their ability to successfully create and manage perceptions. It is important however to remember that the purpose of using the model is to make sure you receive credit for the real brand inside. The strength of a personal brand starts deep inside an individual.

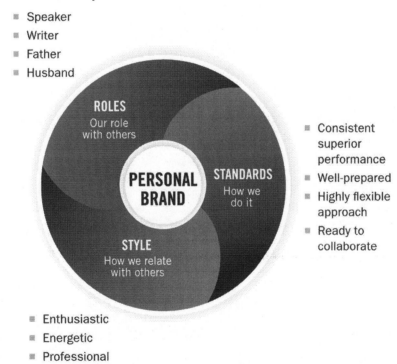

- Speaker
- Writer
- Father
- Husband

- Consistent superior performance
- Well-prepared
- Highly flexible approach
- Ready to collaborate

- Enthusiastic
- Energetic
- Professional

FIGURE 7. Chip Bell's Personal Brand Dimensions Model Brand Tool Box Personal Brand Model © 1989–2008 Brand Tool Box, Ltd.

Now that we have completed the "short course" on personal brand basics, we are moving to the next section in the book, "Designing Your Personal Brand of Making a Difference." In this next section, we will provide you with the tools to develop a personal brand platform, the framework to empower you to consciously and competently build a stronger personal brand.

PART II

Designing Your Personal Brand of Making a Difference

4

Authenticity: The Cornerstone to Building a Strong Brand

Many books on personal brand have been published since we wrote the first edition of *Be Your Own Brand.* A primary focus on authenticity continues to be the one outstanding difference between *Be Your Own Brand* and those that have followed our lead. Authenticity and alignment are two of the most powerful drivers in building a strong personal brand. We know that alignment is the bridge that builds trust in a relationship. Authenticity provides strength to the span that sustains the alignment between two people.

We also know that brands gain their strength from the inside out. Authenticity is a measurement of the strength of one's character, and authenticity is the backbone or substance upon which a personal brand is built. Keep this in mind as you design your personal brand, which must start with discovering and declaring what you believe to be your purpose, vision, and values. Only by staying true to these can you be truly authentic.

So far, we've focused primarily on the external side of what it takes to build a strong personal brand.

Now we're going to turn inside and look at what drives and inspires those people who build strong personal brands.

Values with Value

Our approach to personal branding is based on the premise that values are important. Brands have values. People have values. Most people would say they desire to live according to their values. But in our high-speed, hectic world, many people feel that their values often conflict with those of the world around them. Some, in fact, feel they are being asked—even forced—to compromise their personal values to get along with others or to be successful. "Winning is the only thing" is a common philosophy, along with the belief that the personal costs can be added up later.

We don't believe that. To the contrary, we believe that people can be enormously successful because of, rather than in spite of, their values. When your values align with the values of your peers, your family, your customers, and your employer, life becomes a much more harmonious experience.

And that harmony can only be achieved by being true to who you are. It's achieved by being committed to and holding on to your essential values. Call it "integrity," "authenticity," "being true to yourself," or any number of other things. No matter how it is named, the results are greater peace of mind, a more rewarding life, and an enhanced sense of your own self-worth.

We maintain that a successful brand is an accurate, genuine representation of the substance at the core of either a business or an individual. To receive credit (acknowledgment, acceptance, recognition) for that reality, the business or individual must actively live their brand's values every day, testing them in the "marketplace" of personal and professional relationships and watching how others accept or reject those values. Ultimately, whether a personal brand is strong and viable will be revealed in the depth and breadth of the relationships that do or do not take form.

It all starts with, and continuously loops back to, the way you integrate your values into your life. And as we've emphasized, the objective is not merely to live your values as the bedrock for a strong personal brand, but also to receive credit, to be positively acknowledged for those values from the world around you. Without that credit your commitment to those values cannot be fully realized. The world—as evidenced through your relationships—isn't seeing that vital connection. It isn't seeing the "real you."

In helping you build and maintain a personal brand as a means to success, we cannot stress enough this idea of relationships—of connection. We have nothing against (in fact, we encourage) taking time alone, reading uplifting books, watching motivational videos, or anything else that promotes personal development. But in the end, to succeed, the ability to build deep and meaningful relationships with others is critical.

It's a familiar pattern:

A scientist will work alone for weeks, months, even years, gaining new knowledge and making exciting discoveries inside the lab. But until the results are tested and validated in the "real world," all that time and effort doesn't begin to pay off.

The difference between a garage band and an international phenomenon, or Shakespearean soliloquies recited in the shower or from center stage, is the presence or absence of a connection with a larger world.

The great American poet Emily Dickinson worked for years in an upstairs room, the fruits of her genius carefully wrapped in ribboned packets and stowed in a trunk. Only after her death, when her sister discovered her work and sought to have it published, did her writing begin to have an effect on the world.

Whether you seek to achieve career goals, financial goals, family goals, altruistic goals, or any combination thereof, a strong personal brand will succeed for you only to the extent that you actively and purposefully put it to work in the world around you.

Authenticity: Time to Step Up

The most intimate relationship you have is with yourself. Consequently, a strong personal brand is a powerful way for the world to see and value the authentic you. Therefore, the process of brand building involves a certain amount of introspection.

The dictionary defines "authentic" as "true to one's own personality, spirit, or character." When it comes to relationships, authenticity is what others say they want most from us. We make the most lasting and vivid impressions when people witness us being true to our beliefs, staying in alignment with who and what we really are. That's authenticity.

When you summon the courage to be authentic, the effect is powerful. Trust is built faster and maintained longer when people believe you are being real, rather than putting on a false front to cover up what's really going on inside of you. Authenticity doesn't come easily, however. For, as we have intimated previously, courage is not in abundant supply in our world.

If you stop at this point for a moment, you might hear something inside you that sounds like this: "An inspiring notion, but you guys are just too idealistic. Very noble, but the world simply doesn't operate that way. I would love to be genuine and authentic, but where I work the culture wouldn't support it." It doesn't take long at all for the little but-but-buts to sound like a small engine, an engine on a vehicle going nowhere.

We have evidence that the world *can* work this way. Your friends and family *can* get it. Your boss and any other person with whom you have a relation-

58

ship *can* and *will* develop respect for you. You can and deserve to feel better about what you're looking at in the mirror every morning. But you need to make a commitment—here and now—to work deliberately to make sure people experience you as a truly authentic person.

Close investigation of people with strong brands typically will show they have used authenticity to fuel their success. You can, too. Three very recognizable signposts can guide you on the road to authenticity:

- The first signpost is what you see as your purpose for being in this world. Why do you exist? Why are you here?
- The second signpost describes your vision. What do you want for your life? What are your dreams? What do you want to create?
- The third signpost clarifies your values. What do you hold to be true? What's important to you? What are you willing—and not willing—to do to succeed?

When people are living a life that is purposeless, when they exist with no vision for the future, there is no grounding for their values, no motivation to act, and nothing that inspires the desire to enrich their own life and the lives of those who surround them. Any effort to be authentic in these circumstances, therefore, is a meaningless endeavor.

On the other hand, if you believe there is a purpose to your life, that what you envision yourself contributing to the world is important, that your values have depth and substance and merit, then it's much easier to feel inspired to discover ways to become more effective. When your purpose, vision, and values are expressed as a brand that people find distinctive, relevant, and consistent, you've got something the world shows no signs of ever getting enough of.

First Signpost: Purpose—What Is My Life About?

Purpose is what gives meaning to everyone's life. You can be as metaphysical or religious with this concept as you want to be, but people all want to believe that they matter, that there is a reason for their existence. However individuals reach that realization, the depth of their conviction as to why they are in the world directs the way they think and the way they behave. This, in turn, has great bearing on how they wish and choose to relate to others.

In terms of the practical realities of brand building, the more clarity you have about why you do what you do—your purpose—the greater the chance of achieving your objectives. This clarity doesn't happen automatically, however. As we've pointed out more than once, someone else has a stake in the relationship—and consequently a vital role in determining its ultimate success or failure.

To see the validity of this distinction, consider how these ideas and ideals are applied to the ever more competitive world of business. In the sales arena, for example, it appears to be a "no-brainer" that positive relationships are fundamental to success. For many years, however, sales training has largely consisted of teaching manipulative techniques that, in the name of building relationships, often damage or destroy them.

Even today, if you ask top sales executives, "What is the purpose of a salesperson?" the most common answer you'll hear is, "To close the deal." Yet customers loathe being "closed." In fact, the focus on closing is the primary reason salespeople have developed such a poor reputation.

Ironically, although people resist "being closed," they love to buy. However, they want to buy from someone they trust. In enlightened organizations, sales training has shifted its primary focus from how to close to how to successfully open and build trusting relationships.

And what is the most effective way for salespeople to build trust? To have, first and foremost, a primary purpose: solving the customers' problems and meeting their needs. When customers believe that a salesperson has their best interests at heart, they will give that person the opportunity to earn their business—not just once, but again and again.

In the short term, powerful persuasive abilities may allow you to settle issues with colleagues, a spouse, or a child on your own terms very quickly. But a consistent lack of interest or desire to meet their long-term needs closes down the vital lines of communication that nourish those relationships. As the effects compound, your relevance deteriorates. The result is a weak personal brand.

How people behave toward others, therefore, is driven by what they see as the purpose of their relationships. If they are concerned only with their own agenda, those intentions will get through and be felt by the other person no matter how "smooth" the initiating person is. It won't take long for others to look elsewhere for a person willing to put the other's needs first.

On the other hand, if the initiating person demonstrates a consistent interest in sustaining a relationship that may go on for a long time (perhaps a lifetime), others will experience the person's purpose as being genuinely concerned with the other's needs and desires. The initiator's relevance to the other person's life skyrockets. And as the initiator expresses this purpose and makes a difference consistently over time, his or her personal brand grows stronger and stronger.

Second Signpost: Vision—What Do I Want to Create?

There is something magical about an unencumbered and uninhibited child's approach to the world. David finds his grandson, Evan, a constant source of fascination—and personal brand insights. Not distracted by the responsibilities of parenthood, David has had the luxury of observing Evan's accelerating learning curve and the unbridled joy that accompanies each new discovery.

Evan is no exception to the rules of child development. Even though he has recently reached his teenage years, he still experiences a considerable amount of joy and happiness in day-to-day life without the stresses of the adult world intruding. Being lovingly cared for is, of course, a major reason for that joy. That's the external support a child needs. But something of equal significance is going on in the lives of children—they are constantly involved in discovery and the act of creation.

To create means to bring into being something that has never existed before. For children, virtually everything is a new discovery—about themselves, about the important people in their world, about that world in general. Their unrelenting curiosity ignites the phenomenal growth they experience intellectually and emotionally. They are immersed in that wonderful time where the encouragement they receive allows a vision without limits. Anything and everything is possible.

Of course, eventually the fairy tale is exposed. The unlimited vision of life's possibilities becomes progressively more limited. Some of this is simply a necessary process of developing a practical appreciation for reality—children learning they can't fly like Superman, sing like Pavarotti, or make all of the people and forces around them behave in precisely the ways they want them to.

But some of it also is a result of learning to perceive limits where none exist, of making unconscious decisions that harden over time into barriers the growing child considers more powerful than they may actually be. Those barriers may keep a child from acting when the only thing that's holding the barriers together is a perception in the child's mind.

In his numerous books (including *Repacking Your Bags* [Berrett-Koehler, 2002] and *Whistle While You Work* [Berrett-Koehler, 2001]), career and life-planning expert Richard Leider provides valuable insights into the consequences of lost visions. When someone tells Richard about feeling hemmed in by life circumstances, Richard is prone to ask, "Suppose that an eighteen-year-old walked up to you at this moment and said, 'Here's exactly what you're going to do with the next twenty to forty years of your life.' How would you react?"

Odds are most people would, at best, find such unsolicited advice laughable. At worst, they'd be outraged. After all, what possibly qualifies an eighteen-year-old, a mere teenager, to lay out a meaningful course for anyone's life, including his or her own?

That is precisely Leider's point. For many people, the essential decisions that directed the course they have been on for twenty years or more were based on decisions made when they were about eighteen years old. Unfortunately, from the limited perspective available at that age, those decisions rarely took into account such life-enhancing questions as, What do I believe in? What do I want to contribute? What do I want to create for my life? Rather, the needs of the moment may have focused on more tangible issues, such as pay and security or getting through whatever seemed to be the most immediate crisis they faced. Not the stuff to stir the soul, is it?

Small wonder that the personal brand many people unconsciously develop doesn't cast a very distinct shadow. It has been years—decades, in some cases—since they gave any real thought to what the world they want to be living in should look like, instead of what it does look like.

Whether you have a clear vision of the future you're trying to create for yourself and for the important others in your life—or if it has been years since you've updated the childlike sense of possibilities once so powerful a part of you—your life is meant to be a process of purposeful creation. And it can't be stopped by forces outside of you. It begins again at your discretion, whenever you choose.

Therefore, wherever you are—and however far that is from where you want to be—you can combine the knowledge and wisdom you've gained through the long, hard years with the sense of possibilities you once had, to define a vision that truly represents what you want for your life.

Life is never richer, more full, or more rewarding than when you are moving faithfully and persistently toward a compelling vision. When you are purposefully creating, you become fully alive. That vitality imbues your personal brand with an essential energy that can make it even more viable and attractive.

Third Signpost: Values—What Do I Hold to Be True?

All strong brands, whether business or personal, have at their foundation a clear belief system. Yes, they may have wonderful logos, ads, and package designs; but make no mistake, it's the value provided—which reflects the values within—that people care about and are attracted to. Long term, you don't choose FedEx because of its snappy commercial slogans or UPS because its trucks are painted brown. You choose them because the reliability of their performance is a continuing demonstration of their commitment to what they believe—their values.

In business, organizations with the strongest external brands have the strongest internal values. When an organization's values are clear, they are shared by those within the organization. The result of that clarity and unanimity is that customers respond and relate to those values on a positive emotional level.

Similarly, the values you relate to in a spouse, child, close friend, or respected mentor are beyond considerations of how they look, the position they hold, or the car they drive. You connect to something inside them. To develop a strong personal brand requires very clear values—and the commitment to build enduring relationships that reflect those values.

Brand Values Profile

In the game of life, people are constantly confronted with situations where they might feel pressured or tempted to act in ways that are contrary to their values. Those compromises are judgment calls that often confront people in unexpected ways. But such judgment calls are easier to make in accordance with your values if you've given some thought to those values and how they apply to building your personal brand.

An important part of building a personal brand is identifying your values—what you believe and don't believe, what you hold to be true, what's important to you, what you respect and don't respect, and what you are willing and not willing to do to achieve your goals.

Research conducted by the Minnesota-based Meiss Education Institute finds a strong connection between understanding our most important values and making better decisions—the kind of decisions that help us develop more effective relationships with others. The Institute defines personal values as the inner rules or principles we use to make choices and run our lives. To help people identify their most closely held values, it has developed a Personal Values Profile (at http://www.meisseducation.com/), a portion of which we've adapted here into a Personal Brand Values Profile to help you clarify what you feel and believe strongly—your values.

This survey-style profile has no "wrong" answers. You are not being tested. And no answers are better than others. Rather, this non-psychometric measure indicates personal preferences regarding values. It is designed to help you understand yourself, recognize the issues involved in a situation at hand, and then choose values-based strategies appropriate to the situation.

Through this Personal Brand Values Profile, we'll help you to:

- Identify your top seven personal values.
- Differentiate between your real values (the ones that you actually operate from) and your idealized values (the ones you think you should operate from).
- Anticipate and minimize potential conflicts with others.
- Learn to make better decisions in your work life and personal life, based on your values preferences.

Step One. Read each value and place a check mark in the appropriate column to indicate its relative importance to you ("Not Important," "Somewhat Important," or "Very Important"). Rate all values on the list. Use the "Other" spaces to add values important to you but not included on this list.

Value Description	Not Important	Somewhat Important	Very Important
Achievement (results, tasks completed)			
Adventure (new experiences, challenge, excitement)			
Artistic Expression (drama, painting, literature)			
Balance (proper attention to each area of life)			
Competition (desire to win, to take risks)			
Contribution (desire to make a difference, to give)			
Control (desire to be in charge, sense of order)			
Cooperation (teamwork, working with others)			
Creativity (new ideas, innovation, experimenting)			
Economic Security (freedom from financial worries)			

Value Description	Not Important	Somewhat Important	Very Important
Fairness (equal chance, equal hearing for all)			
Fame (desire to be well-known, recognized)			
Family Happiness (desire to get along, respect, harmony)			
Friendship (intimacy, caring, support)			
Generosity (desire to give time or money readily)			
Health (physical fitness, energy, no disease)			
Independence (self-reliance, freedom from controls)			
Influence (desire to shape ideas, people, processes)			
Inner Harmony (desire to be at peace with oneself)			
Integrity (honesty, sincerity, consistent demonstration of your values)			

Value Description	Not Important	Somewhat Important	Very Important
Learning (growth, knowledge, understanding)			
Loyalty (duty, allegiance, respect)			
Nature (care for and appreciation of the environment)			
Order (organization, conformity, stability)			
Personal Development (improvement, reach potential)			
Pleasure (enjoyment, fun, happiness)			
Power (authority, influence over people and/or situations)			
Prestige (visible success, rank, status)			
Quality (excellence, high standards, minimal errors)			
Recognition (respect, acknowledgment, applause)			

Value Description	Not Important	Somewhat Important	Very Important
Responsibility (desire to be accountable, trustworthy, mature)			
Security (desire to feel safe about things, surroundings)			
Service (desire to assist others, to improve society)			
Self-respect (pride in self, feeling worthy)			
Spirituality (belief or interest in a higher power or God)			
Stability (continuity, predictability)			
Tolerance (openness to others, their views and values)			
Tradition (treasuring the past, customs)			
Variety (diversity of activities and experiences)			
Wealth (material prosperity, affluence, abundance)			

Value Description	Not Important	Somewhat Important	Very Important
Wisdom (desire to understand life, to exercise sound judgment)			
Other:			
Other:			
Other:			

Step Two. After checking the relative importance of all the values, look at those you marked in the "Very Important" column. Your goal for this survey is to refine your list of very important values to the seven you consider most important. Go back through the list and choose the seven values that are most important to you. Record these seven values in any order on the lines below.

Top 7 "Very Important" Values

1. _____
2. _____
3. _____
4. _____
5. _____
6. _____
7. _____

As you review your choices, give thought to whether these are values you actually have and live by or whether they are values you feel you ought to have. You may have chosen a value through a sense of loyalty to an outside influence—family, religion, employer, community, etc. That value, while not to be discounted, may not actually be among the seven values that most commonly and realistically characterize your actions. It is crucial to be honest and realistic, rather than idealistic, in your assessments. Since this is not a test, no one is going to try to impose their sense of "proper" values on you. Give your list one more review and make any changes necessary.

Crystal Knotek has been a client of David's for twenty years. When she was an employee of Northwest Airlines (subsequently merged into Delta Airlines), Crystal's career evolved from starting as a reservations agent to becoming the senior vice president of customer service and airport operations, a position that involved leading over ten thousand employees. Crystal's values were the bedrock for all her relationships, whether professional or personal. She believes that there is nothing more important for an individual than to be true to oneself.

She said, "I want to look forward to coming to work every day. I want to feel passionate about what I do. I want to believe in my company and our commitment to the services we provide. However, as a leader, I want my people to feel the same way. It is my responsibility to make that happen, for myself and for them!"

Crystal never has compromised her values, even putting her career on the line when others in powerful positions disagreed with her decisions. In an industry often, by its nature, adversarial, Crystal built a strong personal brand founded on her authenticity.

Congratulations! You are now in a rare group of people who actually know what is—at the core of their being—important to them. You also have just identified seven key values that will provide the starting point for what we will do next—defining your personal brand platform.

Creating Your Brand Platform: Dimensions and Ethos

You can be any brand you want to be!

Now that we have your attention, let us explain. The possibilities for your brand begin with your values, guided by your purpose, your vision, and your commitment to making a difference for others. Visions and intentions become a reality through well-executed tactical plans. The same is true for building a strong personal brand. You have to develop and manage a plan for your personal brand. At the core of your personal brand plan is your personal brand platform. This chapter will provide you with a pragmatic, simple, and proven framework to define your personal brand platform. After you have defined your platform—steeped in your values—your brand possibilities are unlimited.

Personal Brand Platform Framework

A personal brand platform contains three key elements: a set of personal brand dimensions, a personal brand ethos, and a personal brand promise.

Personal Brand Dimensions: the combination of roles, standards, and style that defines the unique aspects of your personal brand. In this chapter, we're going to show you how to use the model we gave you in chapter 3 to identify and chart the key components of your brand.

Personal Brand Ethos: the single dominant characteristic of your personal brand dimensions.

Personal Brand Promise: a concise, meaningful, and inspiring statement—developed from your brand dimensions and driven by your brand ethos—that sums up the impact a relationship with you will have on someone else. At the core of a solid brand platform is an inspiring brand promise. In the spirit of not overwhelming you, we will provide the background and guidelines for developing a brand promise in chapter 6.

Your Brand Dimensions

Defining your personal brand dimensions and refining them into a personal brand platform involves identifying the roles, standards, and style that go into each relationship people have with you. Since we all learn better through examples or analogies, we would like to introduce you to Dr. David Dunn and his personal brand platform.

Karl first met Dr. Dunn in his position as the head of the Department of Surgery at the University of Minnesota. Under his leadership, the University of Minnesota built a world-renowned reputation as the leader in organ transplantation. Dunn has been credited with making the university's surgery department one of the top in its field in the United States. Surgeons in the department are the only ones in the world performing intestinal transplants involving living donors as well as cadavers; and the surgeons are pioneering work in islet-cell transplantation as a cure for diabetes and in robotic surgery. In addition to being known as a globally respected surgeon, Dr. Dunn is a renowned scientist and administrator, who has published more than four hundred scientific articles and book chapters in the areas of surgical infectious diseases and transplantation. Today Dr. Dunn is the vice president for health sciences at the University of Buffalo, and his reputation as an internationally renowned authority on surgical infectious diseases and transplantation continues to grow. In addition, as a respected health-care administrator, he is providing important leadership in the changing health-care delivery system in the state of New York and the United States.

Step One: Identify the Areas Where Your Roles Matte

Your personal brand dimensions start with what you do, and need to do well, in the context of a relationship. Dr. Dunn demonstrates competencies as the vice president for health sciences at the University of Buffalo, as a surgeon, professor, health-care system administrator, scientist, board member, spouse, father, and as a friend. These are the relationships in which his personal brand will be tested. Write down the important relationships in your life where your roles are on the line.

[space left intentionally blank in the original book]

Step Two: Examine Your Standards and Values

Remember, your personal brand platform strategy connects inside. The soul of your personal brand comes from your sense of purpose, vision, and values. In the context of brand dimensions, your values—not only your top seven, but the whole list—very likely will help you identify standards that begin to differentiate you in your relationships.

Standards also have a performance aspect. Take a moment to reflect upon a situation in which you felt you were at the top of your game. What was it about the way you approached that challenge or problem, or met that need, that revealed an outstanding part of your character? Odds are those are brand standards, too. Was it your responsiveness? Your tenacity? Your clear thinking? Your high energy? The thoughtfulness of your approach? The innovativeness of your thinking? Your unique frame of reference or set of experiences? Your specialized knowledge or expertise? Your willingness to take the lead—or to be a team player or supportive resource? The three to five characteristics that consistently come to the forefront when you review situations in which you performed well are brand standards.

Dr. Dunn's brand standards reflect his commitment to being thorough; his acute attention to detail; his commitment to operate to a very high standard and with an extremely disciplined approach. Let us illustrate Dr. Dunn's brand standards in action, a perception not easy to forget.

In their element—an operating room—you expect surgeons to be organized, meticulous, and obsessed with details. Dr. Dunn doesn't disappoint in that regard. His personal brand begins with his role as a transplant surgeon.

However, what really begins to drive home the strength of his brand are the standards he sets—and lives by—not only inside the operating room, but outside as well. Wherever he is, a level of conscientiousness bordering on perfectionism characterizes everything he does, from surgeries that can last more than eight hours at a time to an hour spent as a committee representative on a task force.

For Karl, Dr. Dunn's distinctive approach to standards and style became personally relevant (and highly memorable) one morning in a boardroom setting. Instead of slides or overheads, Karl likes to use storyboards (slides mounted on chipboard, about eighteen by twenty-four inches) for visual reinforcement. That day, the room was cramped enough that

Karl made his presentation sitting down, without the benefit of the usual easel to hold the storyboards.

As it happened, David Dunn was in the next chair. Karl (who was aware of his impressive medical reputation) made the simple decision, based on convenience, to ask him to hold the boards as Karl finished with them. Without a hint of self-consciousness about position or power, Dr. Dunn readily agreed. The presentation proceeded uneventfully. The task force covered what needed to be covered, and the session finished up.

When it was over, this immensely respected physician handed back the boards—and another piece of anecdotal evidence of what it looks like when people truly live their brands. As he handed back the boards, he said, "Remember, now, they're in reverse order."

The man brings that kind of attention to detail to even the simplest nonwork situations. You'd expect that sort of concentrated focus from a nationally renowned surgeon—but even when he's handling someone else's presentation storyboards instead of his own instruments?

Obviously, that kind of thoroughness—that unassuming approach to "living a brand" every waking minute—made a lasting impression. His personal brand standards and style of thoroughness, attention to detail, perfectionism, humility, and cooperation clearly showed through.

Write down the primary standards and key values that energize your relationships.

[space left intentionally blank in the original book]

Step Three: Define Your Style

Now think of the unique parts of your personality that make an impact on other people when you are at the top of your game. Do people consistently react to your positive attitude? Your humorous demeanor? Your straightforward approach? Your willingness to see the silver lining in every cloud? Your sense of calm? The friendliness of your approach? Your sincerity? Your inquisitiveness? Your sense of whimsy—or your formal, no-nonsense personality?

Dr. Dunn's brand style can be described as humble, collaborative, and friendly. There is no question while watching Dr. Dunn that he is a leader. Like all respected leaders, he is decisive and can be tough when the situation calls for it. But what stands out in his leadership style is the way he brings people along in his decision making. Colleagues are comfortable knowing they are a part of the process of formulating decisions; and they also know that a timely decision will be made, no matter the toughness of the impeding issues. Karl can tell you from personal experience that Dr. Dunn's friendliness and humility are almost astonishing. Dr. David Dunn is a near-perfect clinical specimen of a strong personal brand.

Write down the three to five characteristics that reflect your brand style.

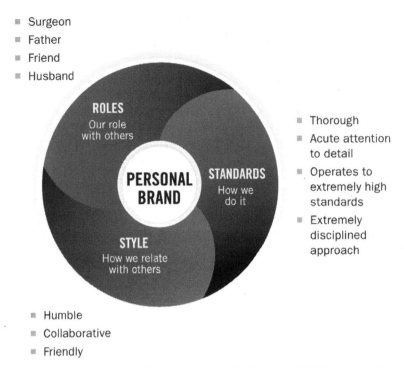

FIGURE 8. David Dunn's Personal Brand DimensionsBrand Tool Box Personal Brand Model © 1989–2008 Brand Tool Box, Ltd.

[space left intentionally blank in the original book]

Dr. David Dunn's personal brand dimensions are shown in figure 8.

Your own model may be less clear at this stage because you're only beginning to gain some familiarity with the model and where to plug in different variables. Here are some considerations that may help you clarify your personal brand dimensions:

Compare your lists of brand standards and brand style characteristics to your list of personal values. Is there a connection? Are your brand standards and brand style characteristics supported by the personal values you proclaim? For example, if one of your brand standards is the knowledgeable way you approach problems, is it supported by a personal value of learning? If one of your brand styles is your friendly approach, did you identify friendship as a personal value? If having fun is high on your style list, is pleasure on your values list?

What do the consistencies and inconsistencies tell you? For each brand standard and brand style, ask yourself, What is it about my approach—the way my values connect to my attitudes and my actions—that makes it more difficult to *consistently* demonstrate the standard and style characteristics I consider (or want to consider) essential to my personal brand?

Use passion as a yardstick to gauge your priorities. Carefully examine each brand standard and style you've identified from the standpoint of your passions. The energy, enthusiasm, and visible personal commitment we bring to what we do help build the distinctive picture of our brand in people's minds. Do you demonstrate so much passion for the characteristics you've identified as important internally that all the people you relate to externally perceive them as distinctive?

The final test is relevancy. As you look at the brand standards and brand style that you're employing consistently and distinctively, assess how well or how poorly they connect with what people seem to need from you. Do the brand standards and brand style characteristics that you identified connect to the standards and style people actually want and expect from you?

Remember that although your brand's roles will vary depending on the nature of the relationship involved—you do, and you are valued for, different things as a parent than as an employer or an employee—your personal brand's standards and style should remain relatively constant (even distinctively so). That kind of constancy is a hallmark of a strong brand. If you're cheerful at work, you should be cheerful at home. If you have the mettle to hold up under pressure as a parent, you should be a good bet to exhibit the same resilience in the workplace.

To build strong brands over the long term, businesses make sure they're applying key brand standards and brand style characteristics in ways that are consistently and distinctively relevant to the competencies involved in each specific brand relationship. You can do the same. Over time, it becomes almost instinctive.

Broken Window Syndrome

In recent years, many cities have become conscious of something called the "broken window syndrome." Often, when a building is abandoned, the first thing that happens is somebody breaks the windows. Those broken windows become a clue, an indicator to others, that the property has become vulnerable.

If the windows are not repaired promptly, a predictable cycle of decline follows—vagrants move in, fires are started, plumbing fixtures are stolen, and so on. The cost of restoring the building to an acceptable quality level rises as its condition deteriorates, making it more likely that the slide into decline will spread to other properties nearby. Cities that use broken windows as an indicator of more serious problems to come intervene more quickly and proactively. The broken windows standard helps them do what they need to do in a more systematic and productive—hence competent—way.

What are the "broken windows" for your personal brand—the expected standards and style you're no longer meeting? They could be something as simple as phone calls not returned, birthdays not acknowledged, promises to attend a child's game or school event that somehow slide by unnoticed. Taken individually, none amounts to a major issue. But as individual instances solidify into habit patterns, the behavior becomes easier to continue, harder to redirect. And the people who are relating to your personal brand begin to modify their expectations of your standards.

Using Your Brand Dimensions

Brands reflect values—they are outward manifestations of what's inside of you. Those inner dimensions can be defined—and need to be—to build a brand for maximum impact. Now that you've identified them and linked them in your Personal Brand Model, you have a powerful tool that can help you build a distinctively relevant and consistent brand. In turn, these dimensions can be used as a yardstick against which to measure yourself and make adjustments to keep yourself and your relationships on track.

Brands, like relationships, are experiential. That's another way of saying that brands build their strength over time, through interactions. The more distinctively relevant and consistent those interactions are, the faster and stronger our personal brands grow.

Unfortunately, most people don't spend much time thinking about the way the interactions in their lives play out. Consequently, their personal brands reflect a random pattern that sometimes succeeds and sometimes doesn't—and which often doesn't seem to respond to predictable norms. It shouldn't be surprising. Here are traits that the people evaluating the brand quality see in such brands:

- A lack of design for distinctiveness or relevancy in what they are trying to be in their relationship with someone else.
- Inconsistency in how they manage the interactions involved in that relationship.
- No promise of value at the heart of the relationship process.

That's why there's no strength in the brand relationship that results.

Your Brand Ethos

As you look at your own Personal Brand Model, what single driving force seems to energize it? If you asked the people who know you best to describe you in just a couple of words, what words or phrases would they come up with? This dominant brand value—either standard or style—is your brand ethos.

Your brand ethos is the single most dominant characteristic of your brand—the one whose nature permeates everything else. In many ways it is what makes you distinctive. It must correlate with your most prized personal value. To determine your brand ethos, review your list of brand standards and style characteristics and decide which of these you are most passionate about and have the courage to consistently and distinctly display—with everyone, all the time. Declaring your brand ethos is an important step for developing your brand promise. We will provide you with a step-by-step process to develop your brand promise in chapter 6.

Now using the criteria mentioned here, write down your single most important personal brand characteristic. My brand ethos is:

[space left intentionally blank in the original book]

To build a strong personal brand, you need to make a conscious effort to manage the relationships in your life so their interactions are memorable for all the right reasons: because they are a distinctive reflection of you; because they are relevant to someone else; and because they are consistent enough that both parties develop a sense of stability and predictability on which to build future interactions.

Now, how do you express the essence of that relationship in only a few words? You're now ready to use your personal brand dimensions and brand ethos to work on your personal brand promise, the topic in chapter 6.

6

A Promise to Be More of Who You Are

A personal brand promise statement will be the single most powerful device you will have in your brand-building tool bag. This short yet inspiring statement will provide the focus you need to apply your distinctive qualities toward making a difference for others. For some folks, their brand promise statement is as succinct as "Insight. Wit. Attitude." Someone else's brand promise may be more descriptive, like "Steady Eddie, getting things done." It does not matter what cadence (and perhaps rhyme) you use with your personal brand promise. What counts most is that your statement reflects who you are and how you desire to engage with others.

A personal brand promise is *for you*—its purpose is to remind you of how you make a difference for others. It is a concise self-expression of how you apply your beliefs and passions for the benefit of others. It has been our experience and observation that when individuals hit the right tone with a brand promise statement, a big smile comes to their face and a real sense of excitement sets in.

Brand Promise to Keep

Every personal brand contains an implicit promise. Some are clearer than others. Some are more ambitious than others. Some are more appropriate than others. But a brand promise should reflect the desire and ability to meet another specific person's needs and desires at a particular time.

A brand promise shouldn't be made lightly. Nor should it be something that comes out differently in each different situation or relationship. Expressed well, it has applications across a broad spectrum. One very important personal brand management skill is to apply your brand promise to the specifics of each relationship, not to change it to suit a new situation. Essentially, you want to make a single brand promise to friends, family, and people at work. A true test of a personal brand promise statement is how well it connects to your brand ethos and how you make it relevant to all the relationships in your life. Consider a familiar business example.

Helloooo, Federal

Think about FedEx for a moment. The FedEx brand promise is "An unrelenting commitment to deliver." As a customer, you may never have heard that promise stated in precisely those words. But if you're working for FedEx—whether sorting packages, driving a delivery truck, setting up airfreight schedules, or buying new computer systems—this promise provides a simple guide for your actions. It can lead to extraordinary responses.

Within FedEx, there are stories of drivers who have gone to amazing lengths to meet the company's delivery commitments: for example, one driver picked up a locked drop box—concrete pedestal and all—to get the packages inside it to the sorting center on time.

You can see that if everybody in a business organization lives out that kind of promise, customers will experience an unparalleled level of reliability. And because the people and systems of FedEx are geared for exactly this result, research consistently shows that the single most important service characteristic FedEx has emblazoned on the minds of customers is reliability. Consequently, "An unrelenting commitment to deliver" qualifies as a very relevant brand promise.

A promise can energize a brand. But the promise doesn't exist in a vacuum. Whether—or how well—it connects to the people to whom it is made ultimately determines if the brand rises or falls. If a brand is a relationship, a successful brand is an intimate relationship. A business can promise its customers something they don't need or want or value. But even if the business keeps that promise, the customers won't care, and consequently the business won't obtain any competitive advantage from all its time and effort. Only when the promise connects to the customers' important needs will the customers value the relationship. Only then does keeping the promise generate real value for the brand.

The same holds true in a personal context. For the important people in your life, your brand promise sums up what you are committed to being and doing on their behalf. Because your brand promise needs to connect to the "real you" as well, it also reflects your values in meaningful ways that you can act upon. The brand promise you make to someone, however silently and implicitly, provides the energy that helps you consistently build distinctive, valuable relationships throughout your life.

A Platform for Promises

In chapter 5, we told you about Dr. David Dunn to show you how to build your own brand dimensions. Dr. Dunn is a prime example of a strong personal brand. His completed Personal Brand Model appears in figure 8 as part of chapter 5.

Dr. Dunn's razorlike attention to detail qualifies as his brand ethos—the single most dominant characteristic of his brand, the brand value whose nature permeates everything else. David Dunn operates to the highest standards; he pays attention to detail at the microlevel; and he exerts hard-as-iron discipline coupled with his collaborative style. From his brand ethos, we can distill his brand promise: "Details drive success." The key is that Dr. Dunn's brand promise is built upon his brand ethos.

There's no magic to creating effective personal brand promises. You'll know when you've got it right—you'll *feel* it. Start with your ethos, and then follow these quick guidelines. Here's how to make your brand promise effective:

- Make it short—five to eight words.
- Give it a voice that is direct and action-oriented, even exciting and inspirational.
- Orient people directly or indirectly to how your brand pays off for them.
- Base it on your brand ethos.
- Reflect how your personal brand provides value to others.
- Fine-tune it through many iterations. Don't be reluctant to tinker and revise.
- Eventually get it to be extremely strong. Don't settle too soon—go for a great personal brand promise that will keep you motivated and focused on your brand strengths.
- Test it with close friends or family—if their eyes light up and they immediately sense how your promise can help you connect with others, it passes the test.

As models, consider these brand promises developed from the various personal brand examples throughout this book:

"Tenacity straight from the heart"

"Steady Eddie, getting things done"

"Enthusiasm that will make your day" (Chip Bell)

Your brand promise states how you will make a difference in relationships throughout your life. The key is knowing how to apply your brand promise in the different aspects of your life—work, marriage, partnerships, parenting, and more. Now, keeping in mind the guidelines in this chapter, write a brand promise. Remember to keep it concise. My brand promise is:

[space left intentionally blank in the original book]

Your Brand Promise at Work

One of the most inspiring and meaningful ways you can express your purpose at work is through the promise you make, however silently, to your customers, your colleagues, and the company at large. In that context, your brand promise not only provides a constant touchstone for your actions, but it also becomes the criterion by which you can judge the success of your efforts. Should you face moments of doubt or indecision, you can look to this promise and ask, Are my actions and decisions helping me keep my promise, or are they hindering me from doing so?

Being clear about your brand promise also reminds you why your work is important and what your responsibilities are to other members of your team. To better apply your brand promise at work, consider:

- What are the key relationships in my working life? The "customers" for your brand at work are those who are most affected by the quality of your work.

- What do these people expect of me? Your actions, and the outcomes that result, are especially relevant in the context of these relationships.
- How can I apply my brand promise so that I am both distinctive and relevant in these relationships? Think of situations where you can clearly demonstrate your brand promise to make a real impact.

Your Brand Promise to a Spouse or Life Partner

For most people, being loved, valued, and appreciated by a spouse or life partner—and loving, valuing, and appreciating in return—are benefits they hope to experience in one exceptional relationship in their lives. If and when they have an opportunity to create that kind of special relationship, success will not be achieved simply by sticking around: it will only be earned by two people who are willing to learn and grow together in a relationship characterized by the utmost respect and concern for each other's well-being. With that in mind, reflect on the following questions:

- What attracts me to this person? What are the affinities between us? Do they spring from similar ideas about purpose, vision, and values? Very likely they do.

- What does this person expect of me? What attitudes and behaviors do they want from me? How am I relevant to this person?
- How can I apply my brand promise so that I am both distinctive and relevant in this particular relationship? Think of situations where you can clearly demonstrate your brand promise to make a real impact on this relationship.

The answers to these questions can help you discover what your spouse or partner wants from you, which can guide you in applying your brand promise in a manner that is meaningful to both of you.

Your Brand Promise as a Parent

Parenting today is an area of great vulnerability. Changing work styles and lifestyles have created significant, often heated, discussions on the appropriate and "correct" way to parent. Reflecting on how you would apply your promise as a parent might lead you to ask:

- Where in childhood are my children now, and what stage are they moving to? At different ages and in different settings, children need different things from their parents.
- What in particular do they expect of me? Your role may be modified by the presence or absence of another parent, or the network of an extended family, or the support (or threats) from the surrounding community.

- How can I remain both distinctive and relevant in these relationships? Committed parents are prepared to adjust their responses to other demands to make sure their children receive the time, affection, lessons, and support they require. Yet they also recognize the need to balance that response in the context of other roles they play, as income-earner, life partner, friend, and—it needs to be affirmed—as a whole and complete individual.

Your Brand Promise as a Friend

Many people find friendship to be one of their most valued privileges. True friends can provide us with genuine compassion in dark times, celebrate our achievements without envy, and laugh at our foibles and eccentricities as we laugh at theirs.

One special aspect of friendship (also true of the bond between spouses or life partners) is the fact that friends are connected by conscious choice, not by accidents of birth or workplace proximity.

Friendships can reach even deeper and more meaningful levels when people learn how to apply their brand promise in those relationships. Ask yourself:

- Whom do I regard as my closest friends? Name names—identifying these individuals will provide insight into their needs and their importance to your life.

- What do they expect of me? Perhaps no other kind of relationship in your life will be characterized by more diverse needs and profiles. This makes looking at each one especially important.
- How do I keep on being both distinctive and relevant in these relationships? Think of situations where you can make a real impact by acting on your brand promise.

He Knew What It Was They Needed to Do

The following description of Norman Borlaug, a Nobel Prize–winning plant scientist, is an excerpt from his obituary in the September 14, 2009, online edition of the *New York Times.*

Dr. Borlaug's advances in plant breeding led to spectacular success in increasing food production in Latin America and Asia and brought him international acclaim. In 1970, he was awarded the Nobel Peace Prize.

He was widely described as the father of the broad agricultural movement called the Green Revolution, though decidedly reluctant to accept the title. "A miserable term," he said, characteristically shrugging off any air of self-importance.

Yet his work had a far-reaching impact on the lives of millions of people in developing countries. His breeding of high-yielding crop varieties helped to avert mass famines that were widely predicted in the 1960s, altering the course of history.

Largely because of his work, countries that had been food deficient, like Mexico and India, became self-sufficient in producing cereal grains....

His Nobel Prize was the culmination of a storied life in agriculture that began when he was a boy growing up on a farm in Iowa, wondering why plants grew better in some places than others. His was also an unlikely career path, one that began in earnest near the end of World War II, when Dr. Borlaug walked away from a promising job at DuPont, the chemical company, to take a position in Mexico trying to help farmers improve their crops....

The next few years were ones of toil and privation as Dr. Borlaug and his colleagues, with scant funds or equipment, set to work improving yields in tropical crop varieties.

He spent countless hours hunched over in the blazing Mexican sun as he manipulated tiny wheat blossoms to cross different strains. To speed the work, he set up winter and summer operations in far-flung parts of Mexico, logging thousands of miles over poor roads. He battled illness, forded rivers in flood, dodged mudslides and sometimes slept in tents....

Dr. Borlaug's initial goal was to create varieties of wheat adapted to Mexico's climate that could resist the greatest disease of wheat, a fungus called rust. He accomplished that within a few years by crossing Mexican wheats with rust-resistant varieties from elsewhere....

By the late 1940s, researchers knew they could induce huge yield gains in wheat by feeding the plants chemical fertilizer that supplied them with extra nitrogen, a shortage of which was the biggest constraint on plant growth. But the strategy had a severe limitation: beyond a certain level of fertilizer, the seed heads containing wheat grains would grow so large and heavy, the plant would fall over, ruining the crop.

In 1953, Dr. Borlaug began working with a wheat strain containing an unusual gene [that created seed heads that] did not shrink, meaning a small plant could still produce a large amount of wheat....

The plants would produce enormous heads of grain, yet their stiff, short bodies could support the weight without falling over. On the same amount of land, wheat output could be tripled or quadrupled. Later, the idea was applied to rice, the staple crop for nearly half the world's population, with yields jumping several-fold compared with some traditional varieties....

By the early 1960s, many farmers in Mexico had embraced the full package of innovations from Dr. Borlaug's breeding program, and wheat output in the country had soared six fold from the levels of the early 1940s....

At the invitation of the Indian and Pakistani governments, Dr. Borlaug offered his advice.... Soon, India and Pakistan were ordering shiploads of Dr. Borlaug's wheat seeds from Mexico....

Gary H. Toenniessen, director of agricultural programs for the Rockefeller Foundation, [calculated that] about half the world's population goes to bed every night after consuming grain descended from one of the high-yield varieties developed by Dr. Borlaug and his colleagues of the Green Revolution.

"He knew what it was they needed to do, and he didn't give up," Mr. Toenniessen said. "He could just see that this was the answer."

The tenacity clearly apparent in Dr. Norman Borlaug's personal brand was a driving force for his work, which made such a profound difference by saving over a billion lives. He single-handedly had a greater impact on solving world hunger than any other person.

Changing the world isn't the standard for a strong brand promise. But choosing to make a difference when you have the chance is a good starting point for all of us.

Moving Beyond Brand Basics

A strong personal brand stands for something. The more clearly defined your brand becomes, the more authentic, lasting, and rewarding the relationships built on it are likely to be. People will see you for who you are, warts and all—but they will see you more accurately and relate to you more effectively as a result of the clarity a well-defined brand brings to a relationship.

By completing the exercises in the previous two chapters, you have created your personal brand platform. Your platform is the core tool that will guide you in developing a stronger personal brand. The key here is that you now have a tactical plan you can use on a proactive basis to create the perceptions that reflect the brand you believe in. In essence, this means you will get credit for who you are. The more credit you receive, the more confidence you gain to become more of who you are.

Hold on now—let's not get too far ahead of ourselves. We have to add a brand assessment framework to our personal brand management tools. Assessing one's brand is the process of finding out how we are actually perceived by others. In chapter 7, we will share a few brand assessment tools that you can use to get a true reading of what your *actual* brand stands for in other people's minds. With that knowledge, you will have a reading on how well the brand platform you just defined is getting through to others.

7

How Strong Is Your Personal Brand Today?

Once you've identified and completed your personal brand platform, an excellent foundation for building a strong personal brand has been established. But that effort will be significantly depleted unless you develop systematic ways to ensure that you are indeed making distinctive, relevant, and consistent connections to the important people in your life; and what you're delivering is truly valued by the other person in each relationship. That feedback, in turn, can help you further refine your brand platform, focus your actions to make sure you are getting credit for your brand dimensions, and gain confidence in your personal brand.

Building Brand Equity

This brings us to the concept of brand equity. A brand relationship is like a bank account. When something you do strengthens the relationship, you're effectively making a deposit. When your actions consistently strengthen the relationship, the balance grows—and accrues interest.

Brands are like that. Successful interactions build the expectation that things will go right the next time, too. If they do, brand equity continues to grow. When something goes wrong, however, the equity in the brand account is tapped and reduced. With an account that is well into the black, even major problems can be encountered and survived without destroying the relationship. But if the balance goes into the red, the relationship can be irrevocably broken.

Think about the emotional nastiness that so often attends a divorce, a firing, or a messy breakup: anger, frustration, bitterness, despair. All of which lead to huge emotional swings. The destruction of a once strong relationship reflects the depth and strength that once was the norm. The very things that once made the relationship strong collapse into and add to the emotional rubble when the relationship fails.

We understand why some people become "relationship shy"—wary of trying to build another intimate personal or professional relationship. Too often, they've built one only to see the structure give way and fall. The Personal Brand Model can help you improve your odds of building something that lasts.

If you look around, you know which people in your life you can unquestionably count on. You may never have thought of that as evidence of a strong personal brand before, but by now you should be beginning to see patterns. You may even find you know someone well enough to sketch out their personal brand platform.

The people that you absolutely know will be there for you—come what may—have proven themselves consistently and distinctively relevant to you in a specific set of circumstances. You know what you can turn to them for, and you have a pretty good idea of how they'll respond. That's a strong personal brand.

A Word about Transactions

To measure the way people interact with your personal brand, you will need to identify the variables involved. Len Berry, author of *Discovering the Soul of Service* (The Free Press, 1999), developed a three-part equation that can help. He notes that in every transaction, participants have three different perspectives from which to judge what is happening:

1. Expectations of what will happen.
2. Experiences of what did happen.
3. Observations of the process of getting from expectations to experience.

All three are important. But in Berry's view, an interesting compounding effect also needs to be taken into account. Rather than simply being added together, Berry's three variables multiply each other. In other words, it's not 1+2+3 that determines how well you're doing, but 1x2x3. Remember, when you multiply something by zero in an equation, the total goes to zero no matter how large the other variables might be.

As Berry's little formula helps explain, everything counts in a relationship. You can go to the doctor and receive competent medical care, but if you notice dirt under his fingernails or her office has a funny smell

106

to it, you start wondering about standards and style. Your observations of the process could keep you from going back and renewing that relationship, no matter how prestigious the name of the medical school on the diploma hanging on the wall. One variable goes to zero and everything zeroes out.

Measuring as a Process

The best businesses measure constantly, and they probe all three areas. In particular, they know how often perception defines reality in our world—what people think they see is what they think they are getting. Consequently, businesses focus a lot of their research efforts on comparing what their customers perceive to what the business wants them to perceive (the intended "reality" of the brand) and also on looking for gaps between perception and reality. Closing those gaps, they've learned, is crucial to long-term satisfaction and staying power. Synchronizing perception with reality becomes a significant focal point for brand-management efforts and justifies frequent, regular measurement.

The questions businesses use in brand measurement are wide-ranging. Is the product creating an image—together with an emotional connection—in the customer's mind? If so, are the image and connection the ones the business intends, or something else? Can they be sustained? Is the brand undervalued? Is it overvalued? Is it being confused with competing alternatives?

All of these questions can apply in a personal context. Suppose you have decided that a key piece of your personal brand promise—remember, consistency should apply in all your important relationships—is that you will always be available and will listen to key people in your life. When you begin measuring, you'll want to find out whether that's something they value. More importantly, do they act as though they believe you will deliver on that promise?

Check the data you are receiving from your own observations. If your children or coworkers think you are there to listen, they will make an effort to communicate with you. And it will be more than surface chatter: they might confide in you or seek your opinions or ask for guidance. Are they doing these things? If not, you need to probe to find out why not.

Bottom line: Remember, everyone has a brand. We're looking at how accurately your brand reflects your values in the minds of other people who are important to you. You must constantly measure your brand to understand what it stands for and how it is impacting relationships in your life.

Ask Around

If the relationship is important, then it's worth managing consciously and deliberately. From your own day-to-day observations, you can begin to develop a sense of whether people are experiencing the brand you are seeking to create.

But don't settle for a single data source—and a subjective one at that. The observations of people you know and trust (spouses, friends, and others) can help you fill in the picture in more detail. Take full advantage of their perspectives on a regular basis. Ask them what they're seeing, and combine their observations with your own to further guide your brand-building efforts.

If you continually check the status of your personal brand relationships (without making a pest of yourself, of course), you will discover how you're doing at reaching your objectives. If you're on target, you will begin to compile "anecdotal evidence" that (to use the earlier listening example) your children or colleagues are indeed using you as a sounding board—they are asking for, and acting on, your insights about what they do, where they go, the dreams they have, and the issues they face.

On the other hand, if there's a gap, where is it coming from?

It could be you. Despite your brand promise to be available and listen, how often are you actually in a physical and mental state where you can give your full attention to someone else? Are you exhausted from other demands? Are you habitually behind the barrier of the computer (or the newspaper), or asleep in front of the television, or so involved in other activities that the important people in your life don't think you have time for them?

It could also be them. Are they able to take advantage of the brand promise you're prepared to make on their behalf? Are they even aware of it? Maybe they're not comfortable confiding in anyone at this point. Or maybe they just haven't received any indication from you that listening is something you are prepared to do and are good at doing. People may be surprised to learn you aspire to be seen as a helpful, supportive listener—which is an example of why helping people connect the dots, so to speak, is such an important part of building productive brand expectations.

He Was Quite Domineering But Honest

The following excerpt taken from Dr. Willem J. Kolff's obituary in the February 13, 2009, *New York Times* describes a fascinating and strong personal brand that reflected his values very clearly in the minds of others.

Dr. Willem J. Kolff, a resourceful Dutch physician who invented the first artificial kidney in a rural hospital during World War II, using sausage casings and even orange juice cans, and then went on to build the first artificial heart, died Wednesday at his home in Newtown Square,

Pa. Dr. Kolff, whose work has been credited with saving millions of lives, was 97....

Dr. Kolff, who immigrated to the United States in 1950, was widely regarded as the father of artificial organs, having proved that biomedical engineers could build all sorts of artificial organs for keeping patients alive. His artificial kidney evolved into modern dialysis machines for cleansing the blood of people whose kidneys have failed, preserving countless lives....

His artificial heart—though it carried the name of a colleague, Dr. Robert Jarvik—is still in use, in subsequent designs, as a bridge to transplantation in patients with heart failure.... It carried Dr. Jarvik's name because it was Dr. Kolff's policy to attach the name of the co-worker who was currently working on any particular model of artificial heart [citation omitted]...

As a young physician at the University of Groningen in the Netherlands in 1938, Dr. Kolff watched a young man die a slow, agonizing death from temporary kidney failure. He reasoned that if he could find a way to remove the toxic waste products that build up in the blood of such patients, he could keep them alive until their kidneys rebounded.

For his first experiment, Dr. Kolff filled sausage casings with blood, expelled the air, added a kidney waste product called urea and agitated the contraption in a bath of salt water....

The concept for building an artificial kidney was born....

In May 1940, Germany invaded the Netherlands. Rather than cooperate with Nazi sympathizers put in charge at Groningen, Dr. Kolff moved to a small hospital in Kampen, on the Zuider Zee (now called the Ijsselmeer), to wait out the war. While there, he set up Europe's first blood bank and saved more than 800 people from Nazi labor camps by hiding them in his hospital. And he continued to work on the artificial kidney.

The device was an exemplar of Rube Goldberg ingenuity. It consisted of 50 yards of sausage casing wrapped around a wooden drum set into a salt solution. The patient's blood was drawn from a wrist artery and fed into the casings. The drum was rotated, removing impurities. To get the blood safely back into the patient, Dr. Kolff copied the design of a water-pump coupling used in Ford motor engines. Later he used orange juice cans and a clothes washing machine to build his apparatuses....

"Dr. Kolff was a visionary who could see farther down the road than most of us," Dr. Don Olsen, a longtime colleague and president of the Utah Artificial Heart Institute in Salt Lake City, said in an interview. "He was quite domineering but honest as the day is long."

Dr. Olsen added, "One thing he did always amazed me: He could come to meetings, see a new procedure or material, then bring it into the lab and find an application for it."...

Dr. Kolff continued to work on artificial organs, including eyes, ears and limbs, until he retired in 1997 at the age of 86, maintaining the same philosophy he had held to when developing the artificial heart.

"If a man can grow a heart," Dr. Kolff always insisted, "he can build one."

Dr. Willem Kolff's personal brand was anchored in his standards of visionary and ingenuity; and his personal brand was supported with his styles of humility and straightforwardness. Applying his sense of curiosity and dedication to medical science, Dr. Kolff made a difference felt by millions of patients. And he surely inspired many colleagues whose personal brands will benefit many more millions in the years to come.

Seek Consistency

When paddling a canoe, you'd be well advised to look around constantly. Whenever a gap opens up between where you're going and where you want to be going, the sooner you spot the deviation, the quicker you can correct your course—and the less radical your adjustments will need to be. Personal brand building works the same way. Use your observations and the feedback you're receiving from trustworthy sources to locate gaps and progress points. Then work systematically to close the gaps. The more consistent you are at staying on course, the more quickly you'll get where you want to go.

Inconsistency is the devil of a strong brand. If listening is a key brand standard for you, make sure your children or workplace colleagues see you model the behavior of being available and an open listener. Respect the confidences of those who have entrusted you with them. If people experience adverse consequences when they take you into their confidence, it might result in others thinking you will react more as a judge, a critic, or a gossip than as a constructive coach or a guide.

Consistency cuts both ways. If you are inconsistent, people—even people very close to you, whom you think should know you better—may not feel they know who you are or what you will do. If they can't count on consistent behavior, if they have to wonder about what you will do in ordinary circumstances, they will find it hard to trust you when the chips are really down, no matter how often or articulately you promise something.

Since actions speak louder than words, if your actions are inconsistent with your words, people will quickly learn to discount your promises. When you truly walk the same path you talk and deliver on the promises you make, they learn to trust you, value you, and count on you to be there for them in the future. Your brand starts to stand for something in their eyes.

Indirect Measurement Tools

Businesses have learned to combine direct and indirect brand-evaluation techniques to build a more accurate picture of the effectiveness of their brand messages. Here are a few indirect measurement tools and some ideas on how you can apply them to keep your personal brand relationships on track.

How far will people go to offer feedback or ideas, including suggestions for improving a brand? A customer who writes to a company about a valued product or service experience is providing evidence of a deeper relationship than someone who checks off a couple of boxes on a handy comment card. Both are placing more value on the relationship than customers (however satisfied they may profess to be) who don't consider it worthwhile to invest the time and energy to offer any feedback at all.

When people take the time to tell you what they like—and what they would like even more—they're making their own investment in furthering the relationship. Pay attention to praise, compliments, and other positive feedback. They are evidence that people are giving you credit for a brand strength, something they value and would like to see continue.

What kinds of complaints do people have—and give voice to? In world-class organizations, a complaining customer, far from being seen as a nuisance, is considered an invaluable resource for product, service, and process improvement. Research suggests that only four percent of customers who have a complaint will actually register it. For every customer who speaks up, another twenty-four suffer in silence—and probably are already looking for new brand relationships. (Meanwhile, they're telling all their friends what a poor job the organization did for them.)

When someone takes the time to let you know you've come up short on your brand promise, use it as a valuable opportunity to retarget your efforts. But remember to examine both sides of the relationship to see where the disconnect originates. Maybe you promised more than you could—or did—deliver, which means you need to focus on consistency. But maybe the intended recipient expected something other than what you actually promised, which means you need to redefine expectations with them. In either case, constructive criticism can help you fine-tune your game.

Now, when it comes to your personal brand, what are people willing to do? Do they return your calls? Do they provide feedback or advance information? Will they add an errand of yours to their to-do list? If a memo or magazine for you was misdirected, would they personally drop it by? Similarly, think about the relationships in which you consistently are willing to go "above and beyond," and ask yourself what that reveals about someone else's strong personal brand relationship with you.

What things do people tell others about the brand? In business, the most powerful form of advertising is word-of-mouth. That's why testimonials are such staples of brand communications activities and why referrals are so highly prized by well-run businesses. Here's a demonstration of how relationship values affect credibility: Researchers have learned that people may say one thing but do something else when the question is phrased to involve only their behavior. But when the question probes the individual's willingness (or unwillingness) to recommend something to a friend, the reliability of the response goes up—as it should—because now they're being asked to react on the basis of a relationship.

When someone comes to you on the recommendation of someone else, find out who sent them—and why. (And remember to thank the referring individual when an opportunity presents itself.) Make sure the person brings realistic expectations; and make sure you meet those or revise them as necessary, because two brand relationships are involved here: the one the person is starting to build with you and the one the person already has with whoever sent them to you.

In this vein, listen to the word-of-mouth you pass along to others. How do you describe people you respect, like, and admire, compared to those who don't rate high on your value scale (and what does the tone of your opinions say about your own brand)? What about their personal brands has or hasn't made an impression on you—and what lessons from your observations can you apply to your own personal branding efforts?

Brand-Building Tools

Beyond measurement techniques, businesses use a variety of tools to define, manage, and extend a brand. Many of them can be adapted to the needs of a strong personal brand as well.

Guidelines. Businesses often create—and measure—specific brand standards and usage guidelines to help people stay true to a brand's values in day-to-day decision making. Your brand platform can serve as a similar "bible" for your brand. In fact, you might want to put your brand platform on a card and carry it with you.

Take a moment to write out some of the standards and guidelines that can strengthen the way your brand is perceived. These may involve the way you dress, the way you speak, how you show interest in others, or a host of other behaviors. Try to keep your list focused on creating a distinctive, relevant, and consistent brand impression.

Remember, little things count a lot. Jim Miller, coauthor of *The Corporate Coach* (HarperBusiness, 1994), was known around the Texas office-supply company he founded for the simple word "terrific." His brand guidelines were so thorough he had even thought through how he would respond to the way people greeted him. Whenever someone, in even the most casual of contexts, asked him how he was doing, he'd never sigh and say, "Oh, fine." He'd immediately reply, "I'm terrific—how are you?" Small wonder he was well known—not only in his company, but throughout the entire office-products industry—for a powerful positive outlook that defined his strong personal brand.

Training. A proven way to improve what you do is to improve yourself. Yet often, in the hustle and bustle of daily life, self-improvement efforts go to the bottom of the to-do list.

Experience is a good teacher, it's true, but the personal equivalent of learning on the job is often a traumatic way to figure something out. Businesses often set a target (sometimes measured in hours, sometimes in courses or certifications or continuing education units) for personal and professional improvement activities. In doing so, they further emphasize their belief that people will become more productive as a result of a regular learning regimen.

Are you willing and able to invest in improving yourself? The two basics are time and money. If you want to improve your skills in parenting, listening, or using the computer, buy a book and make the time to read up on the subject. Lay a foundation for new interests or extend current ones by taking a class at a local college or through community education. On a less formal but equally forward-looking level, try to put yourself in situations where you can practice desired skills and gain useful experience that can be used in other relationships. Volunteer your time and talents at school, in the community, around the neighborhood, with your extended family—but do so with a purpose.

Special Events. Many normal, everyday business efforts are punctuated by special activities—sales, promotions, event sponsorships, and the like—that gain force because they are, by definition, out of the ordinary. Their rarity adds to their significance and impact, not to mention the organization's visibility. Businesses use these opportunities to go out of their way to create special focus on brand dynamics.

Can you reinforce and extend some of your own personal brand values in a similar fashion? Perhaps in the way you celebrate an anniversary or special day in a relationship? Perhaps through public involvement (volunteer work, community leadership, or assisting at school or with the elderly) that reflects a core personal value? Perhaps simply making a deliberate point of saying "thanks" or "well done," or telling someone what they've done to please you? The event doesn't have to be special to become special to someone else. And celebrating it reinforces the value you place on your relationships.

Reward and Recognition. One of the oldest and most true axioms of business is, "What gets rewarded gets repeated." Reinforcing small, ordinary positive behaviors and desired results is every bit as important—more important, in fact—than attacking areas where someone may not always measure up.

It's also more useful than going overboard celebrating exceptional performance that, by its very nature, is never going to be the norm.

Behavioral psychologists say that to be clearly perceived as a positive, rather than a negative, individual you need to make at least three times as many upbeat remarks as negative comments. What's your ratio? If more than one-quarter of your comments are critical, complaining, or corrective—no matter how well intended or needed your responses are—you're going to be perceived negatively rather than positively. If you want your family, coworkers, or friends to value you for your positive contributions, they need to see your positive side in action far more often than the critical side.

Building a strong brand takes time. It involves work. It's an evolutionary process, not a one-time event—as befits the essential nature of a relationship. Don't take things for granted. Question, probe, evaluate, challenge. Then continually improve to build both the strength of your personal brand and the strength of the relationships people develop with you.

Alignment is at the base of building a stronger brand. In chapter 8 we will provide you a context for developing stronger alignment, especially with your employer.

You get to be any brand you want to be. In chapters 4, 5, and 6 we provided you the tools to clearly articulate the brand that describes you best. Declaring your authentic personal brand platform is the foundation for building a strong personal brand.

In the remaining section of the book you will find tools, tips, and insights that will enable you to use the power of alignment to build a stronger brand.

PART III

Using the Power of Alignment to Build a Stronger Personal Brand

8

Aligning to Become a Stronger Brand

When one strives to find and maintain alignment in a relationship, the potential for a strong brand is almost unlimited. Authenticity, as we discussed in chapter 4, is the core strength—or engine—of a strong personal brand. Alignment, however, is what creates the traction and delivers the power for building a strong personal brand.

Alignment is the process of finding common ground for a mutually beneficial relationship. Alignment, especially with the company you work for, does not mean uniformity or changing your personal brand to act, believe, or look like the company. Alignment is about finding that common ground or congruence with your employer that enables you to be more successful professionally while still being who you are.

The power of alignment is one of the most important lessons we have learned for personal brand building. Alignment creates a much larger world of possibilities for individuals and their relationships. Discovering and creating alignment is not a passive endeavor—it takes energy, curiosity, and a bit of humility. Strong personal brands make the effort to discover and maintain alignment in a changing world.

To reap the benefits of a strong personal brand, an individual must personally assume accountability for creating alignment. Alignment is a two-way street: to receive the most from an aligned relationship, one must understand what's important to the other person and the other person must *perceive* the same level of alignment (the relationship is beneficial to them as well). Relationships that are in alignment require less energy to manage and deliver greater benefits for both parties involved.

Individuals behave and respond differently to different people based on their perceived level of alignment with the specific person. Engaged relationships are the most productive and pleasurable. Generally, in closely aligned relationships both people recognize, feel, and highly value the relationship. These types of relationships flourish and are freeing to both entities involved.

Alignment in a relationship is not an absolute; it is a matter of degree. The opportunity to increase the level of alignment exists in almost every relationship. Creating alignment in a relationship requires an active involvement to always improve the connection. In other words, the strength of your personal brand results from you being accountable for establishing and nurturing the alignment in the relationship.

Not all relationships will be completely and fully aligned. Successful and wise individuals have developed the skills to navigate relationships that have relatively lower levels of alignment. We don't always get to pick and choose the relationships we must engage in—whether at work or in our personal lives (irritating bosses or ex-spouse, as examples). Managing the lower level of alignment in these types of relationships will allow us to accomplish our goals with less static and damage to our own happiness and self-esteem.

Alignment in a relationship offers the potential for the most energy to flow between you and others. A relationship that has a great deal of alignment enables you to create value in the relationship by being more of who you are. The more value you create in a relationship, the more encouragement you will receive to be more of who you are. Creating more value for someone else and being more of who you are—that is the amazing payoff for your efforts to create alignment!

Before we go any further on the tactical nature of alignment, we would like to introduce you to a most impressive woman named Temple Grandin. Ms. Grandin is a fascinating example of alignment: she uses its power to make outstanding contributions to the humane treatment of cattle and other livestock, to help calm individuals who suffer from hypersensitivity, and to provide opportunities for promising college students.

The following description of Temple Grandin is an excerpt taken from an article published in the online *Wall Street Journal,* February 23, 2010.

Ms. Grandin—doctor of animal science, ground-breaking cattle expert, [i]s easily the most famous autistic woman in the world....

Born in 1947, she did not speak until the age of four. All of the doctors recommended permanent institutionalization; her father agreed.

But her mother refused and hired a speech therapist and a nanny who spent many hours a week taking turns playing games with her daughter. She insisted that Temple practice proper etiquette, go to church, interact with adults at parties. "I'd be in an institution if it wasn't for her," Ms. Grandin says.

She has always thought socializing was boring, and she famously described herself as "an anthropologist on Mars" to neurologist Oliver Sacks when explaining her interactions with typical people. As a teenager, while her peers fixated on boys and pop culture, Ms. Grandin was consumed with scientific experiments.

Her first major invention, at 16, was a "squeeze machine"—a device she modeled on the squeeze chutes used to restrain cattle that she first saw on her aunt's ranch in Arizona. "I noticed that when the cattle got into the squeeze chutes they got calmer," she says, "so I built a plywood device I could get into that was similar, because I had these horrible, horrible anxiety attacks." The physical pressure calmed her tremendously.

These days, Ms. Grandin is known as much for her professional work—she revolutionized livestock handling equipment—as for her expertise on autism. "I've always thought of myself as a cattle handling specialist, a college professor first; autism is secondary," she says. But she does credit her autism for her unique ability to relate to cattle.

Ms. Grandin wondered what made the animals moo and balk. Kneeling down to see things from a cow's eye view, she took pictures from within the chutes.

She found cattle were highly sensitive to the same sensory stimulants that might set off a person with autism, but were inconsequential to the average handler. They were shockingly simple revelations: light and shadow would stress the animals, as would grated metal drains. Prodding and hollering from cowboys, intended to move cattle along, only alarmed them further.

Her designs reflected these insights. A curved, single-file chute mimicked the cattle's natural tendency to follow each other. She replaced slated walls with solid ones to prevent cattle from seeing the handlers and cut down on light and shadow.

Today, half of the cattle in this country pass through the slaughter systems that Ms. Grandin invented. She's a consultant to companies like McDonalds and Burger King. Yet—and she might well be the only person with these two associations—she's also been honored as a "visionary" by PETA for making slaughterhouses more humane.

In addition to her accomplishments of dramatically improving the humane treatment of animals and helping people with autism and related hypersensitive disorders, Temple Grandin uses all of the proceeds from her publishing and speaking work to provide scholarships to worthy individuals in the pursuit of graduate degrees in animal science.

We don't know Temple Grandin personally, but based on our research it seems to us the distinctive qualities of her personal brand are her tenacity, her hard-working no-nonsense approach, and an undeniable caring nature.

We think Ms. Grandin is an outstanding example of alignment, beginning with how she found commonality between her own autistic perceptions and reactions and the emotional reactions of cattle. She demonstrates extraordinary alignment in how—with her determination and caring—she has evolved from a person unable to speak, into a person who has transformed conversations that span the worlds of slaughterhouses and PETA, autistic people and their speaking relatives, and scientists and their understanding of how the autistic mind works.

Personal Brand Alignment at Work

Although alignment is important in all relation-ships, we focus on alignment between you and your employer's brand in the remainder of this chapter. For most people, finding and being able to leverage some, or a lot of, alignment with their employer is a very important part of building a stronger personal brand.

Businesses rely on the power of alignment to maximize productivity and ultimately deliver the full potential of their business model. A high level of alignment enables an individual to make the most from their talents and energy at work. Strong alignment is also an important driver of overall employee satisfaction. Frankly, not every day at work is a positive experience (an under-statement to be sure). Sometimes you may under-go a period of time (having a boss you don't like, as an example) where you aren't as happy at work.

If you believe there is overall alignment (some or a lot) between your values and the company's values, any consternation, however long it exists, will be more tolerable. Finding alignment with your employer can be a win-win for everyone involved. Your brand will grow faster and the company you work for will likely be more successful because of it.

Most of us spend a large percentage of our time working. In fact, people relate so strongly to what they do that when they describe themselves, it is very often in terms of their work:

"I'm a doctor."
"I'm a manager."
"I'm in sales."
"I'm a teacher."
"I'm a housewife."
"I run a small business."
"I'm in business for myself."

Whether you're salaried, work by the hour, own the enterprise, have a fancy title or not, the purpose of your work is to create value—for yourselves and for others—in both tangible and intangible ways. When you and your employer understand that purpose, an opportunity for dynamic synergy between your personal brand and the business brand is created.

In other words, when the values you stand for and the values your organization stands for align, magic happens. Individuals have more opportunities and a greater desire to succeed, because they are working in an environment that encourages them to be more of who they are, not less. Organizations get more highly committed workers. When your personal values are in harmony with your employer's, you see the success of your employer's brand as the successful expression of your own brand.

All brands are experiential—their strengths grow based on constant interactions. Experiences customers have with a business brand shape their perceptions of it; the experiences people have with you build an impression of your personal brand; and similarly, the experiences you have on the job create your sense of your employer's brand. In the best of circumstances, your values and those of your employer will not only be compatible, but they will also combine in the best interests of the organization's customers. The more alignment among the three—you, your employer, and its customers—the greater the synergy involved. When all three relationships align, powerful things happen.

For many people, however, such perfect alignment is more a matter of wishful thinking than day-to-day reality. They approach work as, well, work—just a job to be endured rather than an experience to be enjoyed. Small wonder so many customers pronounce themselves dissatisfied with what they experience from the businesses with which they interact.

Now that you have a sense of how brands develop and how they can be consciously built to better align with the needs of others, you have a tool kit for gleaning insights into how to make the most of your relationship with your employer. Developing a personal brand won't magically make on-the-job conflicts go away. It can't. But it can help you clarify where your values and those of your employer are in harmony and where they are in conflict. That clarity will enable you to make informed decisions about what you're prepared to do and what you basically cannot do as you devote your personal time and energy to the world of work.

Above and Beyond Linking with Your Employer's Brand

Every savvy business executive knows that great brands get their strength from inside the organization. Brand loyalty begins with the linkage between the values of the employees and the employer. If you clearly understood, or even had to develop, your employer's brand platform, and then if you laid it beside your personal brand platform, how similar or dissimilar would they be? Your values and those of your employer don't have to match exactly, but they should align in key places. In that sense, the comparison may help to clarify some basic understandings. Whom do you do your work for? Whose life is improved because of what you do and how you do it? Do you push papers or expedite the information that improves someone's life? Do you clean rooms (dishes, buildings, computer databases, etc.) or give someone a nicer, cleaner, healthier, better environment in which to live or work? Do you work with words or numbers, or help someone make better sense of their world?

Not only that, but how far do the ripple effects spread as your efforts, in turn, allow someone else to do something for someone—and so on outward from the source? Stopping and thinking about where your work goes and to whom it's important can make all the difference between feeling powerful or powerless, productive or pointless, invaluable or invisible.

In the preceding chapters, you've picked up a lot of useful brand analysis tools. Now is the time to use them to define your employer's brand and determine how closely it aligns with your own. There are two ways to go about the first task. The easiest way is to obtain a copy of your employer's brand strategy. If your employer has not documented a brand strategy, which would not be a rare occurrence, then you will have to surmise one on your own. Of course, it's always possible that you are not allowed access to the company's existing brand strategy. If your employer has not documented a brand strategy or you are not allowed access to it, you will have to infer one on your own.

Let's first focus on determining if your employer already has a documented brand strategy. Let's be clear on what you're looking for. Different companies may call a brand strategy by different names, such as "corporate brand strategy," "corporate identity strategy," "positioning strategy," or "corporate identity guidelines." You may find the brand strategy in one or more of a few different places. Search your employer's intranet site under the corporate identity or brand strategy sections. Another approach is to call or email the corporate communications department and ask them for a copy. If your search is going slowly, ask someone in the marketing department to provide you with some clues to find your employer's brand strategy.

When you find the brand strategy, look for a statement of core values and a brand promise statement. If there is no brand promise statement, you will have to substitute the brand positioning statement. Do not look for a tag line or advertising theme. Tag lines and advertising slogans change often; they don't always reflect the values inherent in the employer brand; and they are designed as "catch phrases" to grab the attention of consumers.

If you are lucky enough to work for an employer who has a brand strategy and gives you access to it, you can begin the process of looking for alignment between your personal brand and your employer's brand. However, if you have not been able to gain access to your employer's core values and brand promise, you will need to estimate or surmise the brand values of the organization. The following process will take a bit of work on your part, but when it is successful, it will provide you with the information you need to compare your personal brand values with the brand values of your employer.

If you don't have a copy of your organization's core values, ask your supervisor or the human resources department—most companies will have a published set of core values. Now compare the statement of core values with the real-world "working values." By working values, we mean the values that are reflected in the way employees (managers and coworkers) interact with each other on a day-to-day basis—the real values that run through the organization. Make a list of the real values that you hold to be true in your organization.

What are your organization's competencies? What standards does it bring to those competencies? What style? Go through the process outlined in chapter 5 to define your employer's brand dimensions. Remember, list only the dimensions that are distinctive and consistent in the way the organization interacts with its customers. Brand dimensions can be positive or negative.

What is your employer's brand promise? Use your employer's brand dimensions as a starting point and follow the process outlined in chapter 6 to derive a brand promise.

Now begin the process of checking for alignment between your personal brand platform and your employer's brand strategy. Compare values, brand dimensions, and brand promises. Where do they align and where do they contradict each other? There is no magic to this process. The more alignment the better. Don't expect perfect alignment, but an alarm should go off if you find none. Take special note of the values that do align. These areas become keystones indicating where you are relevant to your employer and, therefore, have ongoing opportunities to demonstrate the linkage with your employer's brand values and to be distinctive in the employee-employer relationship.

It is our collective experience that most individuals can find at least some, if not a lot of, alignment between their brand and the brand of their employer. It is a matter of degree—the more alignment, the better. We ultimately believe that every individual has the responsibility to work for an organization where there is a great deal of alignment. To stay, knowing there is a lack of alignment, is unfair to you, your family, your fellow employees, and your employer for that matter.

But before you rush to any rash judgments, let's be realistic: If you work in a large organization, your work team and direct supervisor probably are more relevant in terms of alignment. How is your alignment with them? The alignment at this "local level" is most likely more important to your short-term satisfaction and success than is your alignment to the larger organization. Your alignment with the larger organization, however, should have longer-term implications for your career. Now given that many people don't stay employed at any one organization very long, the short-term perspective maybe more relevant. However, we encourage you to seriously consider the power of brand alignment with your *current* employer before you jump at another job offer.

Let us be clear here. When we encourage you to find alignment, we are not saying to change who you are to conjure up some sort of "alignment." Alignment is not the same as uniformity—it's about finding congruence or compatibility. You know we believe that authenticity and alignment are a powerful combination. When you can find alignment with your employer while still being authentic to your personal brand, everyone is better off. In our opinion, encouraging authenticity when there is alignment yields the most from diversity in thought and beliefs.

Thriving instead of Surviving

As Temple Grandin demonstrates, most people have a lot more power than they think they have. Someone else may define what you do in the course of the day. But how you do it is in your hands. We've encountered strong personal brands in all kinds of business situations and settings—across counters in post offices, in the drive-through lanes of fast-food restaurants, in real-estate offices and hardware stores, hospital rooms and classrooms, and sitting in airline seats about as far removed from first-class as you can get while still being inside the plane.

In *The Eagle's Secret* (Dell Publishing, 1998), David used research garnered from over six hundred organizations to show the contrast between individuals who seemed to merely survive every day and those who thrived—to demonstrate the far-reaching effects even small actions and unconscious attitudes can have on our life and work. Survivors focus on work as labor, he noted. Thrivers focus on work as a laboratory: a place to learn, grow, and create. You know thrivers when you see them on the job. Clear signs reveal that they're engaged by their work, not enraged by it. Consider these other ways thrivers approach work:

- Thrivers have a global perspective—they appreciate that major forces are transforming the world of work.
- Thrivers anticipate change rather than merely trying to keep up. This means continually adapting, learning, and growing.
- Thrivers seek to maximize their contribution—they are inspired by a strong sense of purpose.
- Thrivers take responsibility for their careers—they believe in self-empowerment.
- Thrivers work in harmony with others—they respect and honor differences.

And, we would add, thrivers have strong personal brands.

Every impression you make, and every impression someone else uses to build their perception of your brand, is important. Every chance you have to be passionate is a chance for you to be more of who you are. If you're in a place where you can't engage and be truly committed, you are swimming against the currents or, at the very least, treading water. The potential for your life is slipping away minute by minute. Every time you compromise what you believe in, you've built the kind of brand impression you don't want.

In every part of your life, you have opportunities to grow your brand or to lose it. Never, ever, ever forget that. The point is, you're at work for eight hours a day—maybe more. You have to find a way to make those hours work with your brand, not against it or in spite of it. Otherwise, those hours truly will be drudgery—something you didn't want to do yesterday, don't like to do today, and don't look forward to doing tomorrow. Life's too long to live and work that way.

It's your brand. It's your life. Using the power of brand alignment will enable you to get more out of all of the relationships in your life. Holding yourself accountable for seeking and nurturing alignment is a very important step in becoming a stronger brand.

9

Personal Brand Building Has Gone Social

The power of social media cannot be underestimated as a tool for personal brand building. At the same time, the hype associated with social media should be tempered by how you use these powerful digital tools. Personal brand building with social media tools is like learning to use a chain saw—if you don't use it wisely, you may cut off the wrong limb. There is no question that these tools have created a whole new world of brand-building possibilities, unmatched in their power.

For those skilled in using social media tools and who are purposeful in their use, the results can be exhilarating. Others find social media to be intoxicating and the impact on their personal brand can be unpredictable and potentially arresting. To be a social media Luddite is a mistake. We are strong advocates of using social media tools for personal brand building.

Let's be clear: We will not be providing you the ins and outs of how to use specific social media tools. We assume you're already using these tools.

IRL and URL Working Together

Interacting in the social media world is *one* of the tools in your personal brand-building tool bag. As we have discussed earlier in the book, consistency is paramount in building a strong brand. Without a concerted effort, it is easy to inadvertently create inconsistencies in the way one is perceived based on digital interactions and real-world interactions.

Some individuals seem to make a distinction between their interactions and relationships created in the social media space and how they interact more directly with individuals. For the sake of discussion, we call that distinction "IRL and URL." IRL ("in real life") stands for one's real-world personal brand, and URL is our shorthand term for one's online personal brand. In a perfect world, the perception one creates in the social media space, that is, URL, would be coordinated and would reinforce one's IRL personal brand. An analogy would be someone communicating over the phone in a similar manner to how they talk in person. But the sophistication of social media tools creates a far more complex and powerful interactive experience that requires a more proactive effort to ensure consistency.

Some people make a conscious effort to synchronize their IRL and URL personal brands. These savvy individuals use the power, leverage, and reach of social media tools to build an even stronger brand. Other individuals, however, are not as conscious or proficient in coordinating their IRL and URL interactions. These folks are clearly underutilizing the potential of social media tools to build a stronger personal brand.

One of the promises of social media is to use the power of digital technologies to create a community of friends and associates who benefit from having an ongoing conversation and exchange of information. And when your URL interactions reinforce your IRL personal brand, you gain the brand strength that comes from consistency. More importantly, a coordinated brand-building effort will enable you to build a stronger personal brand with a much larger network of people that is impossible without the leverage of digital technologies and the power of social media. Think URL and IRL, not URL versus IRL.

A Platform for Social Media

Your personal brand platform is a tool that will encourage consistent brand building in the social media space. In particular your personal brand dimensions (brand standards and style) define the perceptions that best describe your brand. Focus on making sure that the interactions you create in the social media space echo the dimensions of your personal brand. The personal brand platform is a tool that will enable you to boost the brand-building power of the social media tools you use.

Online dating services clearly qualify as one of the "super apps" of the Internet. Let's face it, there is a temptation to "airbrush" one's image a little in the competitive world of dating. Consider a person whose personal brand dimension is honesty or integrity. If this person is using Match.com or eHarmony.com , for example, to find a significant other, it will be important to create the perception that represents his or her true personal brand. To ensure that the important brand dimension of honesty and integrity comes through, the person must ensure all images and descriptive words accurately reflect this dimension.

Success-driven business professionals must be particularly proactive and conscientious about making sure their presence is well represented in the professional segments of the social media space. As an example, when it comes to talent recruitment, the social network is becoming an important nexus connecting employers and prospective employees. The recruiters in the most innovative companies are bypassing typical recruiting agencies and using professional social networks like LinkedIn to proactively search for the best candidates whether or not the person is looking for a new job. In fact, these progressive recruiters constantly review the professional social network for future candidates, anticipating important future talent needs.

Bottom line for business professionals, the social media world is a new mandate and a powerful tool for building a strong personal brand in the professional social network. What are the professional implications for those whose URL brands are not consistent with their IRL brand? As an example, a person's communication in the URL world could be in such conflict with his or her employer's brand or policies that it might place the person's job in jeopardy. In contrast, think of the power of using social media to represent your personal brand to advance your career. What kind of words do you use in your profile? How about the words you use to leave comments to news articles or on blogs? How do the images in the social media space fit with your brand?

Your personal brand platform provides a set of guidelines for you to get the most brand-building power from using social media tools.

Using Social Media to Make a Difference

Making sure there is consistency in the perceptions you create in the social media world is in some ways a strong defensive strategy. The real opportunity is to proactively use social media tools to build a stronger brand. The primary brand-building strategy is to use the power of social media to make a difference.

Karl's daughter is very active in RAGOM (Retrieve a Golden of Minnesota), a program that rescues and rehomes golden retriever dogs. Her volunteer activities cover the gamut of transporting the dogs from their substandard conditions, finding foster-dog parents, raising money to cover vet bills, and finding permanent homes for the forlorn dogs. Social media is at the nucleus of all these activities. Kathryn uses her vast social network to leverage RAGOM's social media activities. That's taking the power of social media to another power. Of course, when she needs to, she buttonholes Karl to use his network to raise needed cash in particular situations. That's using the power of the social network to make a difference. Does the power of social media help strengthen her personal brand? Yes! Does it impress upon other people her caring nature (one of her brand dimensions)? Yes. Could she have made such a big difference without social media? No.

There are many opportunities in one's professional life to use social media tools to make a difference and build a stronger personal brand. The next time someone you know is looking for a job, make the extra effort to use your network or insights to help move his or her job-search journey further down the path. Do you take the time to pass along an article or RSS feed that may interest a colleague or someone you are informally mentoring? Helping someone build a stronger brand will do wonders for strengthening your brand. When you are facing a challenge in your job, how often do you apply the "crowdsourcing" feature of the professional social media tools you use?

Using Social Media Tools with Intent

Social media tools are powerful and easy to use, which is why we need to be smart and purposeful in capitalizing on that power to build a stronger personal brand. Note, we didn't use the term "harness the power of social media": that's because the social media space cannot be controlled. The power of a network increases exponentially as the number of people (nodes) goes up. The exhilarating nature of this power is the interactions that happen between all the people without your direct energy or control. The risk is all the interactions that take place without your direct control.

Developing and executing a plan for social media can create a powerful tool for building a stronger personal brand. Ignoring or having no plan will result in missed opportunities or—the worst case—in perceptions being created that detract from the strength of your personal brand. Personal brands are built using personal plans; one size does not fit all. Following are a few questions that will help you develop a plan for using social media to support building a stronger brand.

• **What social media tools should I be using?** The tools you use say something about your personal brand. Think of it as co-branding. Each social media tool has its own brand. Facebook is perceived very differently than LinkedIn, for example. Its target audience, what people are saying about that media tool, and how many people use it—these determine the brands of social media tools. Make a list of all the social media tools you currently use. Classify them as to whether they are being used for personal or professional purposes. Next, rank them by how much you use each one. Does your current use of these tools enable you to strengthen your brand in your personal life as well as your professional life? Have you registered to use certain social media tools, but are not actively using them? The tool might be out of your mind, but it is not out of others' sight. Does a dormant social media tool have dated information representing your personal brand? Which tools are you willing to stop using?

The point we are trying to make is that you should have a plan and reason for using each social media tool. As an offensive strategy, make sure that you are using the tools that can proactively build a stronger personal brand. As a defensive strategy, make sure your personal brand is not floating around haphazardly in the social media universe. Deciding which tools to use is one of the few things you can absolutely control in the world of social media.

• **How much time am I willing to spend using social media tools?** The power of social media is directly related to how much and how well you use a tool. Most people are busy and don't have a lot of excess time to actively engage in the social media space. Don't spread yourself too thin. For example, if you choose to write a blog, how often will you update it? Or if you use microblogging tools (e.g., Twitter), are you using the tool to make a statement that has little relevance and lacks impact? Or could that same energy be used to submit content that is directed at building your personal brand? Personal brand building is about quality interactions, not quantity.

• **How do I make my brand distinctive, relevant, and consistent while using social media tools?** Be thoughtful about the content you write when using social media tools. Deliver content in a way that resonates with your brand dimensions. If one of your brand standards is fun, then once in a while inject humor into the statements you make. If being thoughtful is one of your brand standards, make sure the words you use are factual and presented in a well-constructed manner. Be careful not to be more distinctive in the social media space than you are in the real-world space. Don't try to be a bigger personality than you really are. It's easy to push it too far on a keyboard.

Make sure the content you write is relevant to your audience, not centered solely on you. Be sure that the content you submit is relevant to the nature or purpose of the social media tool, too. For example, be careful not to submit too much personal-related content on your professional social media platforms. Adding a personal element to your professional brand can be a powerful brand-building activity—just make sure that the content is relevant and interesting.

Making a comment on a professional social media platform that you are going on a family vacation is not likely relevant to many of your connections.

Work hard to present a consistent, yet relevant voice to the target audience of your social media networks. Make sure your tone and content are consistently presented across personal social media networks and professional platforms.

• **How will I measure the strength of my brand in the social media network?** It is important that you take the time to see how your brand is being perceived in the social network space. An easy way to assess how you are projecting your brand platform is to periodically review the content of all the social media tools that you use. There are also services available to scan the Internet universe to assess your total presence, what you are projecting, and what others are saying about you. Don't be shy about asking your close friends how they perceive your presence on a social media platform.

• **Who should be a part of my social media network?** Remember, we are known by the company we keep. Having more people in your social media network is not always better. Be very judicious when deciding to add a "friend" or "colleague" to your network. It is too common for people to accept an acquaintance or old friend who they really don't know. The other person may turn out to be someone who casts a poor reflection on your personal brand. For example, an associate of ours was asked by an old high school classmate to become his friend on Facebook. Without thinking about it, she accepted the request. Later, when she accessed his Facebook page, she was stunned to find out she was connected to someone who is involved in pit bull fighting activities.

To strengthen your brand, be proactive in adding to your social media network people from whom you can learn or with whom you can make a difference. Eliminating someone from your social network is not easy for most of us, but it needs to be done. Being careful when adding people to your network can prevent your having to go through the stress of having people who may detract from your brand.

• **How will I defend this comment?** Always take ten seconds before you hit the return key. What you have posted is *never off the record* in the social media universe. Count on the fact that whatever you place on a social media platform will find its way to places you had not planned on. Another thing some people find out the hard way is that comments you make in the social media space can last forever and people will find them. There are numerous examples of highly talented professionals whose careers were dinged or cut short because of a comment that is lingering in a social media network. Of course there is the often-repeated advice to young people to mind what images of them and comments of theirs are placed on social media sites, because these could impact their career or even their ability to get a job in the company or industry of their choice.

Let's be clear, social media tools are one of the most powerful personal brand-building tools created in our lifetime. Also keep in mind that social media is only one tool for building a stronger personal brand. The role of social media in strengthening a brand will differ for each individual. To not proactively use these tools is shortsighted. To overweight their importance is easy to do. Creating a consistent personal brand image is "table stakes" for operating in the social media universe. Using social media tools to make a difference for someone else will build a stronger brand in ways you may not have imagined.

10

The Courage to Live Your Brand

The personal brand you create will become a dynamic presence in your life. But to remain strong, it must be renewed every day. It must become a part of everything you do.

On some days, those objectives will be easy to achieve. On other days, you'll face situations that will challenge your ability to stand by the sense of purpose, vision, and values you've chosen to center your life on. You'll also encounter times when your brand promise will be severely challenged.

At times, your brand building will seem to be on hold—when life tries to lull you into a state of complacency, even apathy. Whether the seas are rough or calm, your brand needs to be strong enough to ride out the waves and keep moving in the direction you've chosen.

We want to leave you with one last concept from the brand builder's dictionary: brand moments. Those are the times when your unique combination of roles, standards, and style will be put to the test—when you'll have a chance to be found distinctively and consistently relevant to someone else. In those moments, your brand will shine. Or fade.

Brand moments are opportunities to dramatize the important dimensions of your brand in ways that add memorable clarity to the way you make and keep promises and commitments. Often these moments will be encountered unexpectedly, but still you can prepare for them in advance. Think about the possible scenarios in which your brand may be tested. Where are they likely to come from? How should your brand respond to remain true to your values and its roles, standards, and style? Under what circumstances will you willingly take on greater risk or responsibility? How far "above and beyond" are you prepared to go if new conditions create an opportunity for an out-of-the-ordinary response?

The essence of living a strong personal brand is recognizing and managing those moments—however important or ordinary they may appear—on behalf of your brand's immediate and long-term interests. Just as a business brand needs champions, so too, does your personal brand need you to consciously build the relationships through which you and your brand will thrive and succeed.

Some days, that will be a simple matter of doing what comes naturally within the context of those relationships. And you'll find in those moments that you're not alone: When you have a strong brand, you'll attract allies. The people to whom your brand matters will be drawn to it. They'll support it. They'll fight for it—and for you.

Other days, you'll be called upon to go above and beyond what you usually bring to the relationship. Your values will be put under the microscope. Your commitment—to yourself, your brand, and the people who depend on you and matter to you—will be tested. Experience tells us that personal brands gain a disproportionate amount of brand equity during times of stress and distress. It is at these meaningful times that personal brands show their true colors. These types of situations can be fraught with high risk or potentially adverse outcomes. And the result often has higher and often longer-term impact. How your brand contributes or not will leave a big impression on others—the perception that adds to or detracts from your brand equity.

Everyday life presents people with constant opportunities to refine their brands in the crucible of simple acts: To add to the gossip or defend a friend (or someone who isn't a friend). To wallow in the worst of a situation or look for the best in it. To take the easy way out or stand by their brand. To indulge a bad habit or reinforce a good one. To take a little more than they need or give a little more than is required.

The continual—and ultimately life-defining—tests of the values that underlie your brand can arise out of exactly these kinds of simple, everyday dilemmas. To receive credit for your beliefs means dealing with the ordinary as well as the extraordinary, rising to the challenges as well as keeping on an even keel, acting forthrightly in situations you control, and reacting capably in situations you don't control.

Brand moments offer tremendous potential to define, strengthen, and communicate your brand and its values. You can either dread these moments for the challenges they represent or look ahead to them as the opportunities they are. You can even practice responses for how you'll handle them. Either way, when the pressure's on—and the spotlight is on you—you'll face a moment of truth for the brand you want to be.

In the first edition of *Be Your Own Brand* we offered ten working principles that you can use to proactively and consistently build a stronger personal brand. But now, we must add an essential and most important eleventh principle—as you will see:

1. Develop and refine your personal brand platform. The objective of building a strong personal brand is to receive credit for who you are and what you believe. The process can be enhanced considerably if you give yourself time to think through the implications of that quest and identify the resources you bring to it before the proverbial "last minute."

That's not as easy as it may sound. Most of us have so many demands on our time and attention; we seldom take a break for reflection. We're running from the instant we roll out of bed to start the day, to the time we flop back in, totally exhausted, at day's end. It's not surprising that we don't make time for some systematic personal assessment. Yet without some periodic self-maintenance, even what we might consider our most cherished beliefs can get a little fuzzy around the edges.

Throughout this book, we've scattered detailed snapshots of the brand roles, standards, and styles of people we've used as exemplars of strong personal brands. From their stories and the charts, you'll see the essential pieces of a brand puzzle emerging. We encourage you to use these pieces with the Brand Tool Box Personal Brand Model to develop your own personal brand platform. What roles are you called on to supply in the relationships that matter in your life? What standards can you build on? What style characteristics help fill in the subtle dimensions of your brand?

2. Be "brand proud." If you want to be perceived as a strong personal brand, you must decide what you stand for, and then you must be that to the nth degree. You have to work from a firm values platform, not shifting sand. When your vision and values are put to the test, your roles, standards, and style need to align and capably represent the authentic you.

The values profile in chapter 4 is one important resource to draw on. Revisit it periodically and watch for signs of both consistency and change. Use the "top seven" process to track your strengths and the shifting priorities others present through the brand relationships in your life. Then consciously make these values a part of your character.

Your values must be valuable to you, so stand up for them. You can't "kind of, sort of, most of the time" believe in your values or act from them only periodically when the conditions seem right. You must live those values consistently, courageously, even dramatically, on a day-to-day basis. How else can the people who know you and depend on you trust that they can count on you, no matter how convenient or inconvenient the moment?

3. Audit your brand promise. From your personal brand platform and your detailed understanding of your bedrock values, you should find it increasingly easy and natural to crystallize the essence of what you bring to the important relationships in your life. Develop a compelling, passionate, and motivating brand promise, and use it as the focal point of your actions.

Continually revisit and refine your promise in the light of new experiences and insights. Listen carefully to what people say, and watch what they do in response to your efforts. If you're achieving the desired effect, what can you learn from this success to increase the odds of building even greater value with each new contact? If you're coming up a little short, what do you need to do to close the distance between where you are and where you want to be?

Take private time to reflect. Get feedback from others. Don't guess about the status of important relationships. Boil your intentions down to a promise you will keep, and then make sure you're keeping it.

4. Be authentic. Strong personal brands are built by making conscious, conscientious choices based on what you truly stand for. And once those choices are made, you have to be willing to stand up for them when the world doesn't immediately line up and sing your praises. Really great brands, business or personal, reflect the values and convictions of their originators as demonstrated over time.

Good or bad, the parents, teachers, bosses, colleagues, friends, and—if you're lucky—lovers who have shaped the course of your life have shown you a connection between their actions and their soul. The people who value their relationships with you have the same feeling about you, the same kind of emotional bond as you have. It's not an easy bond to create. But the payoff for the effort can be profoundly worthwhile.

5. Make sure the signals you send convey relevance to others. Being a strong personal brand absolutely requires sensitivity to the needs of other people. Brands are relationships. Your brand image exists in someone else's head. You don't create it in a vacuum. To create a clear image of being distinctive, relevant, and consistent in response to someone else's needs means establishing a clear channel for communications—then sending out something that truly meets those needs.

For many people, finding a balance between "me" and "we" can be a troubling issue in personal brand management. You may have a strong sense of the person you want to be, the signal you want to send. But you may feel anything from a vague discontent to an outright unhappiness because the connections you expect as a result aren't in place, or aren't holding up over time, or aren't validating the sense of value you believe you represent.

Check the frequencies. Could your brand messages and behaviors lack enough passion and energy to be heard? Or could they be indistinguishable from all the other "noise" in the spectrum of daily life? Is your message distinctive? Are your values in harmony with your roles, standards, and style? Are you "on the air" all the time, or only broadcasting periodically—and not on a regular schedule?

Fine-tune the signals you're sending, and you may find that your brand begins to connect in the way that you want it to.

6. Consistency. Consistency. Consistency. If you're acting from a coherent belief system, people should see consistency in your actions and learn to value you accordingly. And although they don't know why you do what you do, they will interpret your actions as a projection of a consistent belief and value system, and will credit you in that context.

In business, it's axiomatic that "everything counts" for the customer. For your brand, as well, everything counts. Pay attention to the consistency of the impressions you make. Keep your head in the game. Great brand relationships aren't built on one-time encounters. They are created, nurtured, and solidified by conscious long-term effort in which even apparently inconsequential details are given attention and are managed consistently toward a desired objective.

Pay attention to what you do and how you do it. What's "normal" for you in the relationships you value? Why is that normal behavior both distinctive and relevant to someone else? What can you do to improve those aspects of your behavior while enhancing your consistency? When you find the right places to be, map them out and develop them into strong, healthy environments—for everyone involved.

7. Make sure your package reflects your contents. Your brand is a perception stored in someone else's mind. This means that everything they see, hear, sense, feel—even wonder about—is added to the composite picture they carry around with your name under it. If you could see that picture, would you recognize yourself?

People learn with their eyes much faster, and with much more lasting impact, than they do with their ears. Researchers find that well over half the impact we have on another person comes not from our words but from our tone of voice and, more importantly, our body language and the other elements that make up our visual package.

How you look and the way you talk can be great tools for establishing a strong personal brand. Be personal brand–savvy with the way you look and the way you communicate. For example, notice how impeccably any U.S. Marine is dressed and put together.

That "starched" look and demeanor goes a long way to reinforce the discipline that is the core component of the Marine brand platform. By comparison, imagine Albert Einstein, a wrinkled, disheveled-looking, eccentric genius. His look reinforced the perception that all his energy was being focused on making the next theoretical breakthrough in physics; he didn't have time to comb his hair or make sure his shirt fit. His presentation certainly reinforced his particular brand platform of intelligence.

Your "package" should be an accurate reflection of what's inside—make sure the impressions you're creating are the ones you want to be creating. Set an impeccable standard for everything that adds up to how others perceive you. Your smile, your facial expressions, your posture, the way you use your hands and your eyes, the words you choose, your tone of voice, how you're dressed, and the environment in which someone finds you—all contribute to your brand identity.

8. Brands are known by the company they keep. As you become clearer about your values and the way you want them to connect to others, you will gain a useful standard for evaluating the people in your life. Being a strong brand means people recognize that certain values are essential to you being yourself. Your friends—your true friends—are attracted by those values. They don't try to make you into something you're not. They see you for what you are, and they value you because what you are is relevant to their lives. That cohesion builds a kind of community far more powerful than anything defined by a zip code.

So make conscious choices about the significant (and insignificant) others in your life. Surround yourself with a supportive community of friends and associates who share the vision and values important to your brand.

This won't be as hard as you might think. Strong personal brands, just like strong business brands, attract people with similar beliefs. People really do know it (whatever "it" is) when they see it, and they move closer or farther away accordingly. When you're clear about who you are and what you will do on someone else's behalf, people will either accept that or look for a more relevant connection somewhere else. Those who value the strengths you have will want to associate with you. Those who don't, won't.

You can consciously guide that continuing selection process. In the light of brand relationships, take a good look at the people you habitually surround yourself with. Brands get energy from the likeminded brands around them. They can lose energy when they're surrounded by incompatible brands. Evaluate your relationships. Are the personal brands in your life nourishing your brand or stunting its growth?

9. Find alignment between your personal brand and your employer's brand. One axiom of coaching is to put people in positions where they can succeed. The baseball manager who sends the light-hitting utility infielder out to bat cleanup is as much to blame as anyone else when the hapless player strikes out with the bases loaded. The ballet producer who pushes the ninth swan from the left to center stage and expects a prima ballerina performance worthy of the Bolshoi needs to shoulder much of the responsibility when the audience starts shifting uncomfortably in their seats.

The same holds true for you and your brand—but you're both the performer and the coach. Give yourself a fighting chance. Put yourself in positions where you can succeed. Take yourself out of situations where you are doomed to fail—or worse, may have to compromise your values to get by. Knowing your values, understanding your strengths and weaknesses, and polishing your relationship skills avail you nothing if you don't take the initiative to make sure you're the right person in the right place.

None of us live in a perfect world. Odds are we never will. A lot of the strong personal brands around you are based on values you don't share. We all have to accept that the people attached to brands and values we disagree with may be fully content that those brands reflect their inner souls. The workplace is one arena in which those conflicts tend to surface.

If your employer doesn't share your values, you can stay and struggle—and likely get beaten down from your unappreciated efforts. Or you can go to work for people who appreciate the values you bring to work with you and who will align them with their own for everyone's greater success.

10. Start counting relationships as part of your asset base. We believe real success, for a life as well as a brand, is defined in terms of relationships. What really enriches everyone's lives are the people who love them, like them, trust them, rely on them, enjoy being with them, or even simply tolerate them.

There's a huge difference between building a web of mutually rewarding relationships and having a large number of "friends" or connections in the social media space. To build a strong and viable relationship with someone calls for a form of selflessness that even mature people must occasionally struggle to attain.

If you decide who you are and the kinds of relationships that are important to you, and then act consistently on that vision and those values, you are being fundamentally true to yourself. And if you are fundamentally true to yourself, you will discover a treasure trove of riches and accomplishment.

11. Go social or go home. Maintaining a presence in the "new" social networked world is not an option—it's a "brave new world" of opportunity. Social media presents a very powerful tool for building a stronger personal brand. Certainly many of the working principles presented in this chapter apply in the socially networked digital space. At the same time, many new rules apply to this new reality. For example, a CEO-level client of Karl's was being considered for a new CEO position of a prominent industry trade group. Before making the final offer to this highly qualified individual, the company leaked ("sources say") to a major trade publication that this person was being considered for the position. Many people read the article online and posted their opinion of this successful individual, some positive and many negative. Some may judge the company's approach as unethical, others as shrewd. Nonetheless, it is now a common way, once primarily used in major league politics, to gather feedback about a candidate before finalizing a deal.

Who is linked to your digital brand? Remember, we are known by the company we keep. How often do you conduct a scan of your digital brand presence? There are firms you can retain to do a periodic scan for you. Knowing that recruiters are proactively looking for a database of qualified candidates, what are you doing to make sure that your profile in the social network keeps you in the running for the best new positions? Without such a profile you may never hear about these attractive opportunities. Do you really believe there is a personal social network and a professional social network? Think again.

The Art and Soul of a Personal Brand

We believe that by choosing to make a difference for others you get to be more of who you are and more of who you want to be. The distinctive value you can choose to provide for another person during brand moments creates a clear perception that your brand made a difference. You created equity in that relationship. The stronger your brand becomes, the more productive relationships you have to enable you to achieve what's important to you. By making a difference along the way, you get to know the feeling that being more of who you are really does matter. The stronger your brand, the larger your world of possibilities becomes.

What happens now is entirely up to you. This was never intended to be a feel-good book. It is intended to be a do-good book. We can't tell you what's right for you in any given situation. Only you can determine that. But the key is to make those determinations, not on the basis of your own needs, but on how you can make a difference for someone else.

Creating and living a strong personal brand is for the benefit of others, not only for yourself. It's one of the best investments you'll ever make. The world needs strong brands. It respects them. It relies on them. If you can be one, we'll all be the richer for it.

Works Cited

Berry, Leonard L. *Discovering the Soul of Service: The Nine Drivers of Sustainable Business Success.* Free Press, 1999.

Blakeslee, Sandra. "Willem Kolff, Doctor Who Invented Kidney and Heart Machines, Dies at 97." *New York Times,* February 13, 2009, Health section. Accessed August 13, 2010. http//www.nytimes.com/2009/02/13/health/13kolff.html.

Gillis, Justin. "Norman Borlaug, Plant Scientist Who Fought Famine, Dies at 95." *New York Times,* September 14, 2009, Energy & Environment section. Accessed July 26, 2010. http://www.nytimes.com./2009/09/14/business/energy-environment/14borlaug.html.

Leider, Richard J. and David A. Shapiro. *Repacking Your Bags: Lighten Your Load for the Rest of Your Life.* 2nd ed. San Francisco: Berrett-Koehler, 2002.

Leider, Richard J. and David A. Shapiro. *Whistle While You Work: Heeding Your Life's Calling.* San Francisco: Berrett-Koehler, 2001.

McNally, David. *The Eagle's Secret: Success Strategies for Thriving at Work & in Life.* New York: Dell, 1998.

Miller, James B. and Paul B. Brown. *The Corporate Coach: How to Build a Team of Loyal Customers and Happy Employees* (New York: HarperBusiness, 1994).

The Power of Purpose, film produced by David McNally. http://www.davidmcnally.com/the_eagles_store.htm l.

Temple Grandin, film directed by Mick Jackson (HBO Films, 2010). http://www.hbo.com/movies/temple-g randin/index.html.

Weiss, Bari. "Life Among the 'Yakkity Yaks': The Renowned Inventor on How the Insights She Gained from Her Own Autism Fueled Her Career." *Wall Street Journal,* February 23, 2010, Opinion section. Accessed August 13, 2010. http://online.wsj.com/article/SB10 001424052748703525704575061123564007514.htm l?KEYWORDS=Temple+Grandin.

David McNally is the best-selling author of *Even Eagles Need a Push: Learning to Soar in a Changing World, The Eagle's Secret: Success Strategies for Thriving at Work and in Life,* and *The Power of Encouragement.* An award-winning film producer, David has produced two highly acclaimed, inspirational films,

The Power of Purpose and *If I Were Brave.* David's books and films have been translated into twelve languages and released in over twenty countries.

Recognized as one of the most dynamic and inspiring speakers in the world today, David was recently elected into the prestigious Speaker Hall of Fame.

Throughout an extensive international business career that has included assignments in South Africa, Europe, and the South Pacific, David McNally discovered that inspiration is the foundation of all great accomplishments. But it was the alignment of that inspiration with processes, products, and people that enabled a company to achieve sustained business success.

Now as the president of TransForm Corporation, David and his team consults with companies to help them develop Purposeful Leaders, create Inspired Organizations, and build Iconic Brands.

Clients that have praised David's work include Abbott, Ameriprise, Carlson Wagonlit Travel, Delta Airlines, Fidelity, Gartner, lia sophia, Merrill Lynch, Otto Bock, Perkin Elmer, Pulte Homes, Thrivent Financial, and many more of the world's most respected companies.

Contact information: TransForm Corporation, 9717 Colorado Rd., Bloomington, MN 55438, USA. Web site: www.transformcorp.com; Telephone (952)835-0300; E-mail: info@transformcorp.com

Karl D. Speak is a global expert known for his pragmatic and unconventional approach to using brand as a leadership platform for customer-centric employee-engaged cultures. Karl's in novative work on personal brand and internal brand building has been implemented in companies in twenty-three countries. Karl is a best-selling author and sought-after speaker. As an accomplished presenter, Karl's energetic style and wide-reaching knowledge of brand make him a favorite speaker with audiences around the world.

Brand Tool Box, Ltd., the company he founded in 1984, is the global leader in developing and implementing internal brand-building programs. Through Brand Tool Box, Karl has implemented his contemporary approach to brand management and internal brand building with a wide range of corporate clients. Clients such as 3M, American Express, AT&T, BASF, BMW, Cabela's, Cargill, Consumers Energy, EDMC, FedEx, Honeywell, IBM, ING, Mosaic, Motorola, Securian, Skandia, Sony Corporation, St. Jude Medical, Syngenta, Target Corporation, The Scotts Company, *The Wall Street Journal,* Toro, and Walgreens have benefited from Karl's consulting and internal brand-building programs.

Karl has taught in the MBA programs at University of Minnesota, Saint Thomas University, and has been guest lecturer at University of Westminster in London, Capella University, and ESADE University in Madrid, among others.

Contact information: Brand Tool Box, Ltd., 510 First Avenue North, Suite 605, Minneapolis, MN 55403. Website: www.brandtoolbox.com; Telephone: (612)338-5009; Fax: (612)338-4714; Email: info@brandtoolbox.com

⬢ Berrett–Koehler
B̄K̄ Publishers

Berrett-Koehler is an independent publisher dedicated to an ambitious mission: *Creating a World That Works for All.*

We believe that to truly create a better world, action is needed at all levels—individual, organizational, and societal. At the individual level, our publications help people align their lives with their values and with their aspirations for a better world. At the organizational level, our publications promote progressive leadership and management practices, socially responsible approaches to business, and humane and effective organizations. At the societal level, our publications advance social and economic justice, shared prosperity, sustainability, and new solutions to national and global issues.

A major theme of our publications is "Opening Up New Space." Berrett-Koehler titles challenge conventional thinking, introduce new ideas, and foster positive change. Their common quest is changing the underlying beliefs, mindsets, institutions, and structures that keep generating the same cycles of problems, no matter who our leaders are or what improvement programs we adopt.

We strive to practice what we preach—to operate our publishing company in line with the ideas in our books. At the core of our approach is stewardship, which we define as a deep sense of responsibility to administer the company for the benefit of all of our "stakeholder" groups: authors, customers, employees, investors, service providers, and the communities and environment around us.

We are grateful to the thousands of readers, authors, and other friends of the company who consider themselves to be part of the "BK Community." We hope that you, too, will join us in our mission.

A BK Life Book

This book is part of our BK Life series. BK Life books change people's lives. They help individuals improve their lives in ways that are beneficial for the families, organizations, communities, nations, and world in which they live and work. To find out more, visit www.bk-life.com.

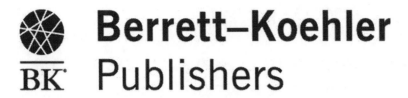

Berrett–Koehler
Publishers

A community dedicated to creating
a world that works for all

Visit Our Website:www.bkconnection.com

Read book excerpts, see author videos and Internet movies, read our authors' blogs, join discussion groups, download book apps, find out about the BK Affiliate Network, browse subject-area libraries of books, get special discounts, and more!

Subscribe to Our Free E-Newsletter, the BK Communiqué

Be the first to hear about new publications, special discount offers, exclusive articles, news about bestsellers, and more! Get on the list for our free e-newsletter by going to www.bkconnection.com.

Get Quantity Discounts

Berrett-Koehler books are available at quantity discounts for orders of ten or more copies. Please call us toll-free at (800)929-2929 or email us at bkp.ord ers@aidcvt.com.

Join the BK Community

BKcommunity.com is a virtual meeting place where people from around the world can engage with kindred spirits to create a world that works for all. BKcommu nity.com members may create their own profiles, blog, start and participate in forums and discussion groups, post photos and videos, answer surveys, announce and register for upcoming events, and chat with others online in real time. Please join the conversation!

Books For ALL Kinds of Readers

At ReadHowYouWant we understand that one size does not fit all types of readers. Our innovative, patent pending technology allows us to design new formats to make reading easier and more enjoyable for you. This helps improve your speed of reading and your comprehension. Our EasyRead printed books have been optimized to improve word recognition, ease eye tracking by adjusting word and line spacing as well as minimizing hyphenation. Our EasyRead SuperLarge editions have been developed to make reading easier and more accessible for vision-impaired readers. We offer Braille and DAISY formats of our books and all popular E-Book formats.

We are continually introducing new formats based upon research and reader preferences. Visit our web-site to see all of our formats and learn how you can Personalize our books for yourself or as gifts. Sign up to Become A RHYW Registered Reader.

www.readhowyouwant.com

Made in the USA
Las Vegas, NV
21 January 2023

66022115R00116